this book belongs to

All rights reserved. No part of this book may be reproduced in any form or by any electronic or mechanical means including information storage and retrieval systems, without permission in writing from the author. The only exception is by a reviewer, who may quote short excerpts in a review.

Cover designed by Maria Smirnova

KALEIDOSCOPE MANDALA

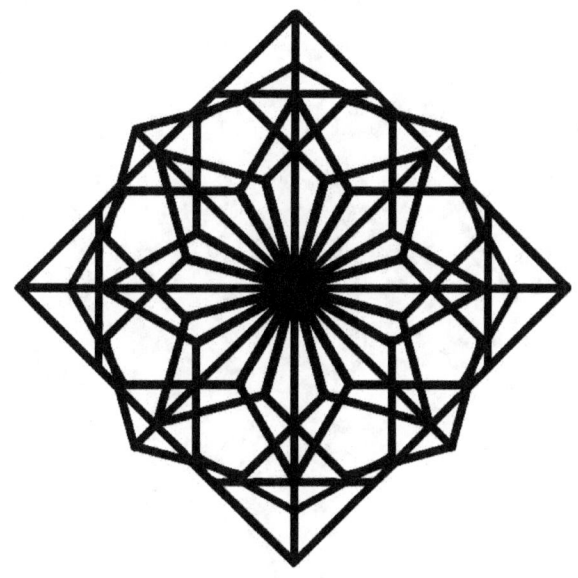

Artwork by

Maria Smirnova

Visit my Instagram at
www.instagram.com/best.coloring.books

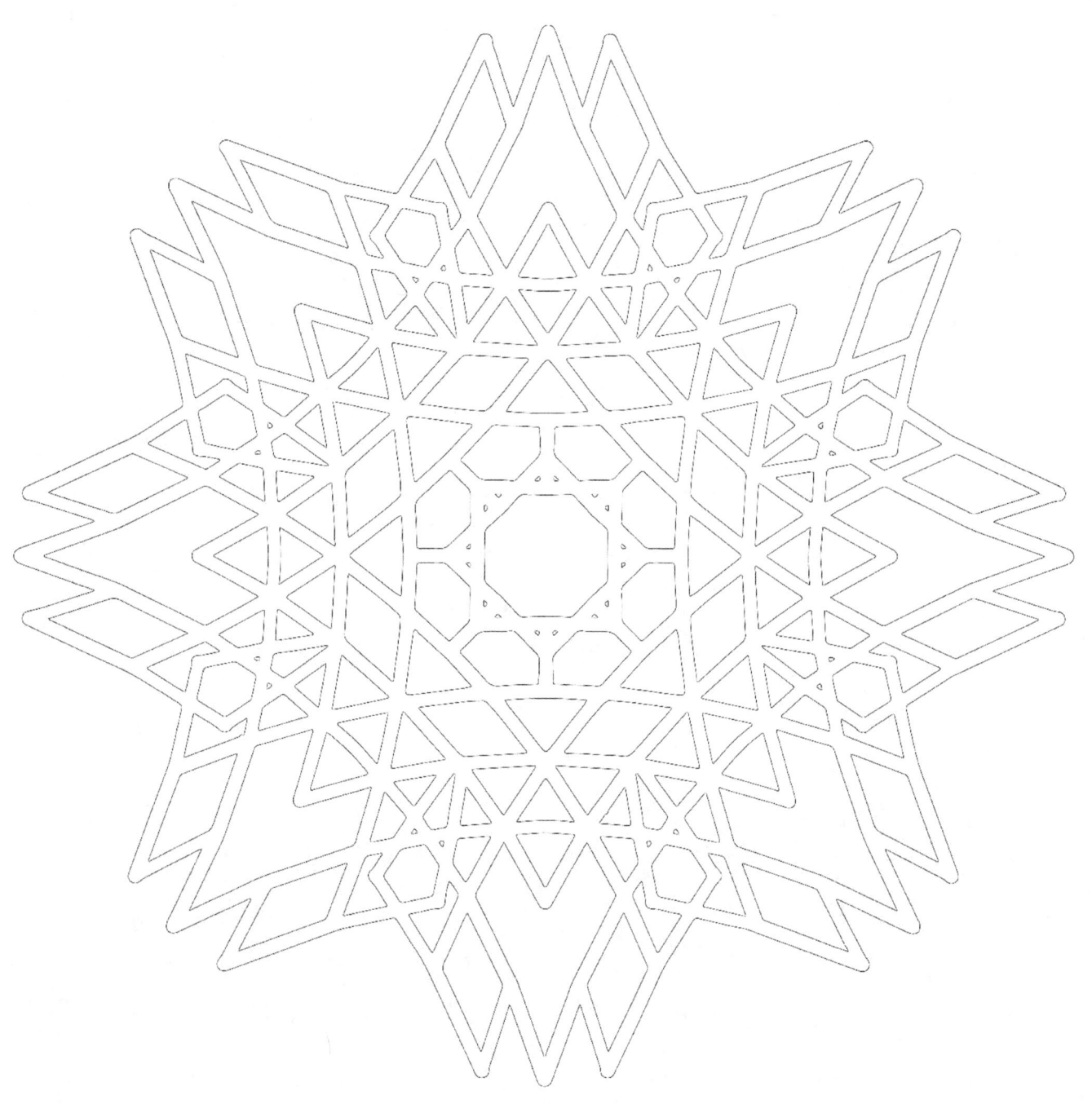

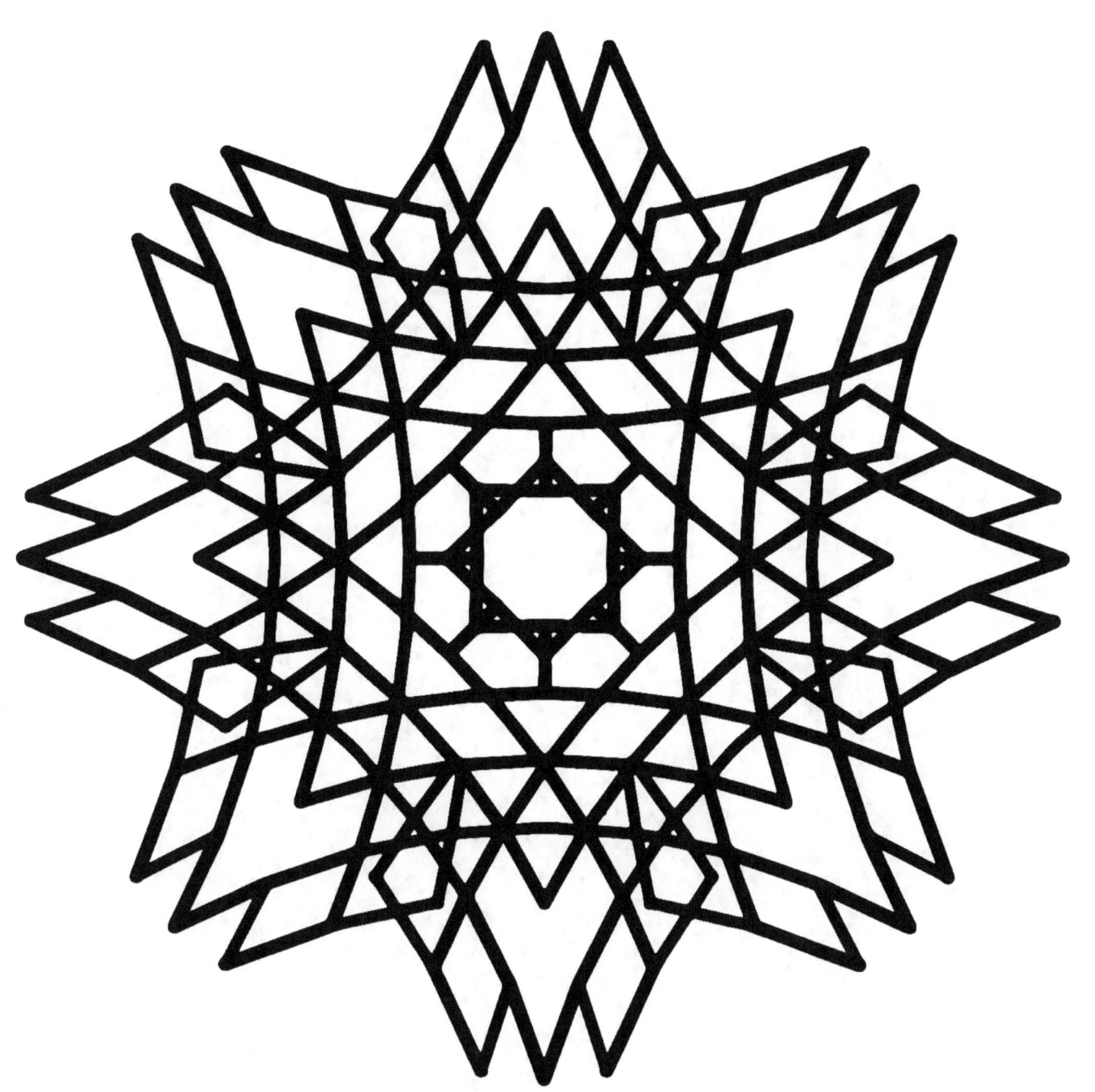

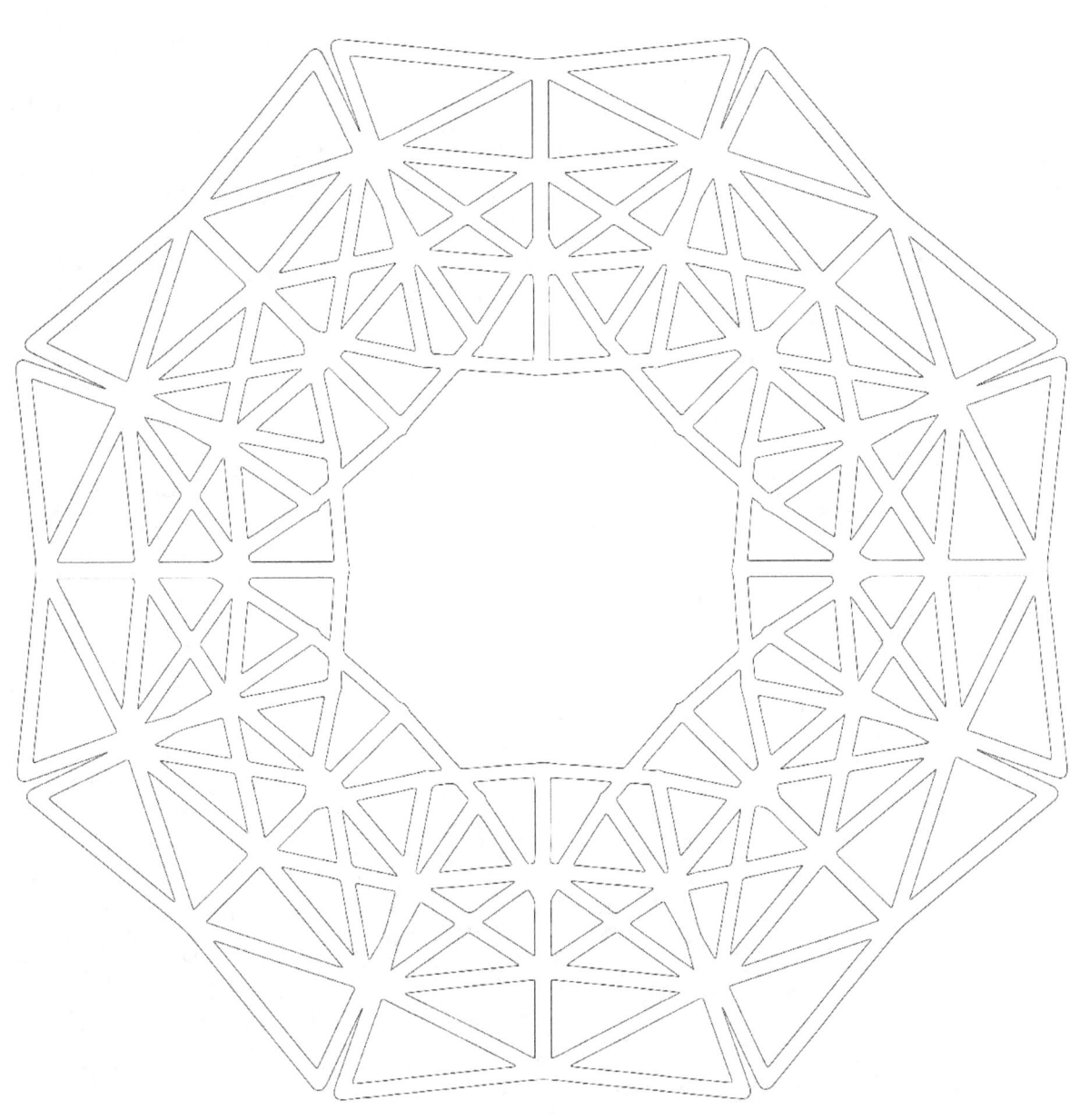

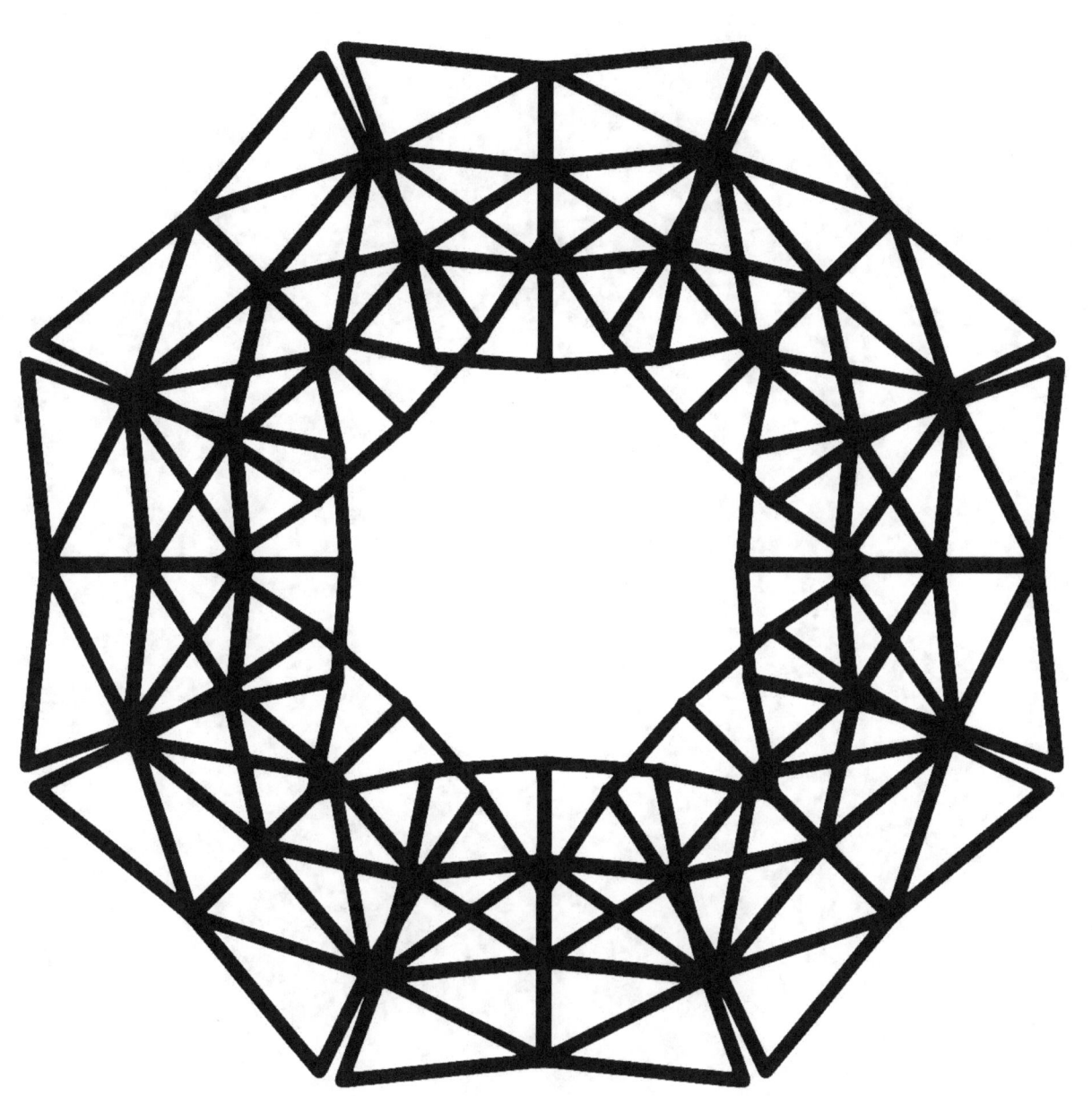

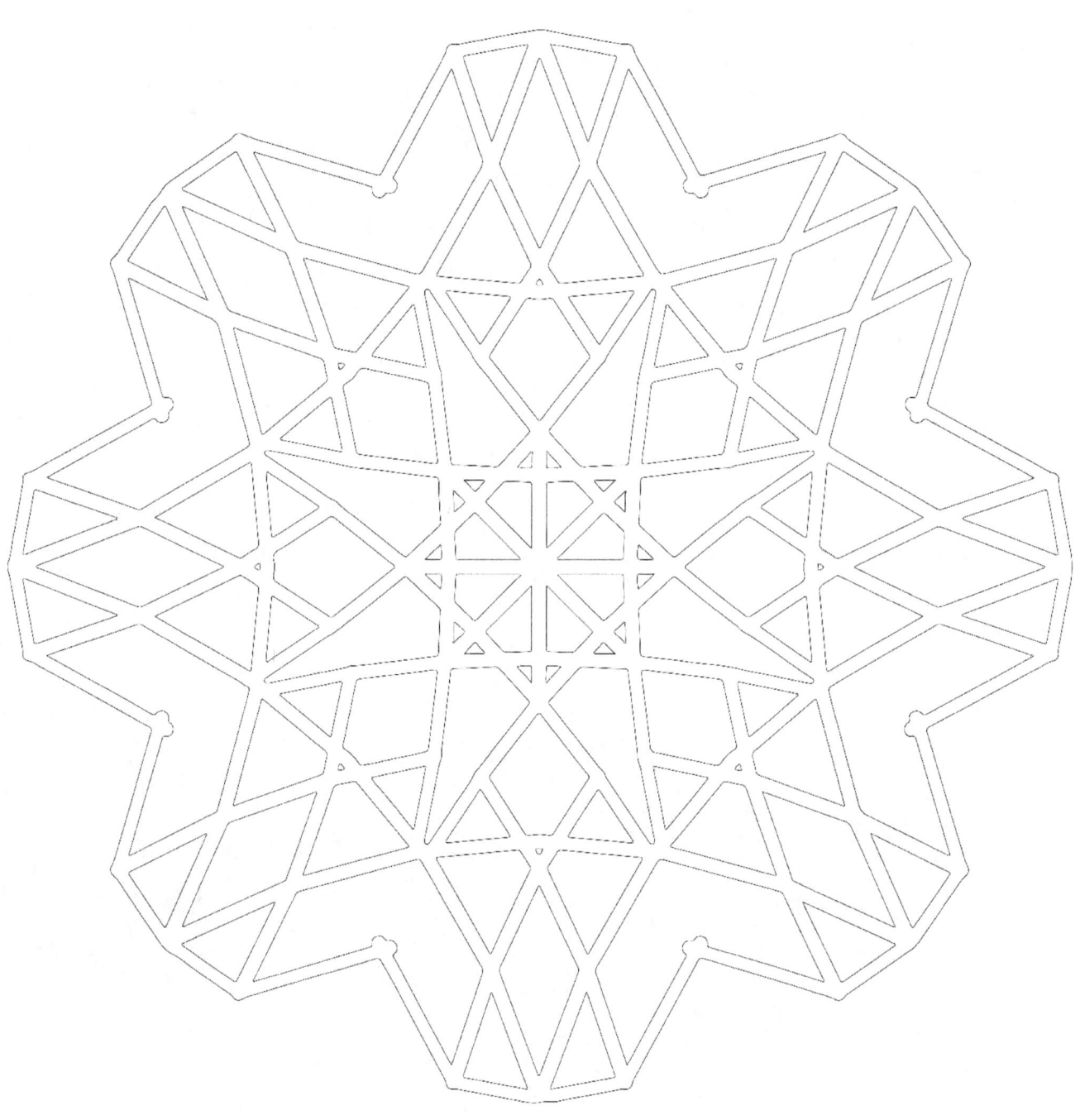

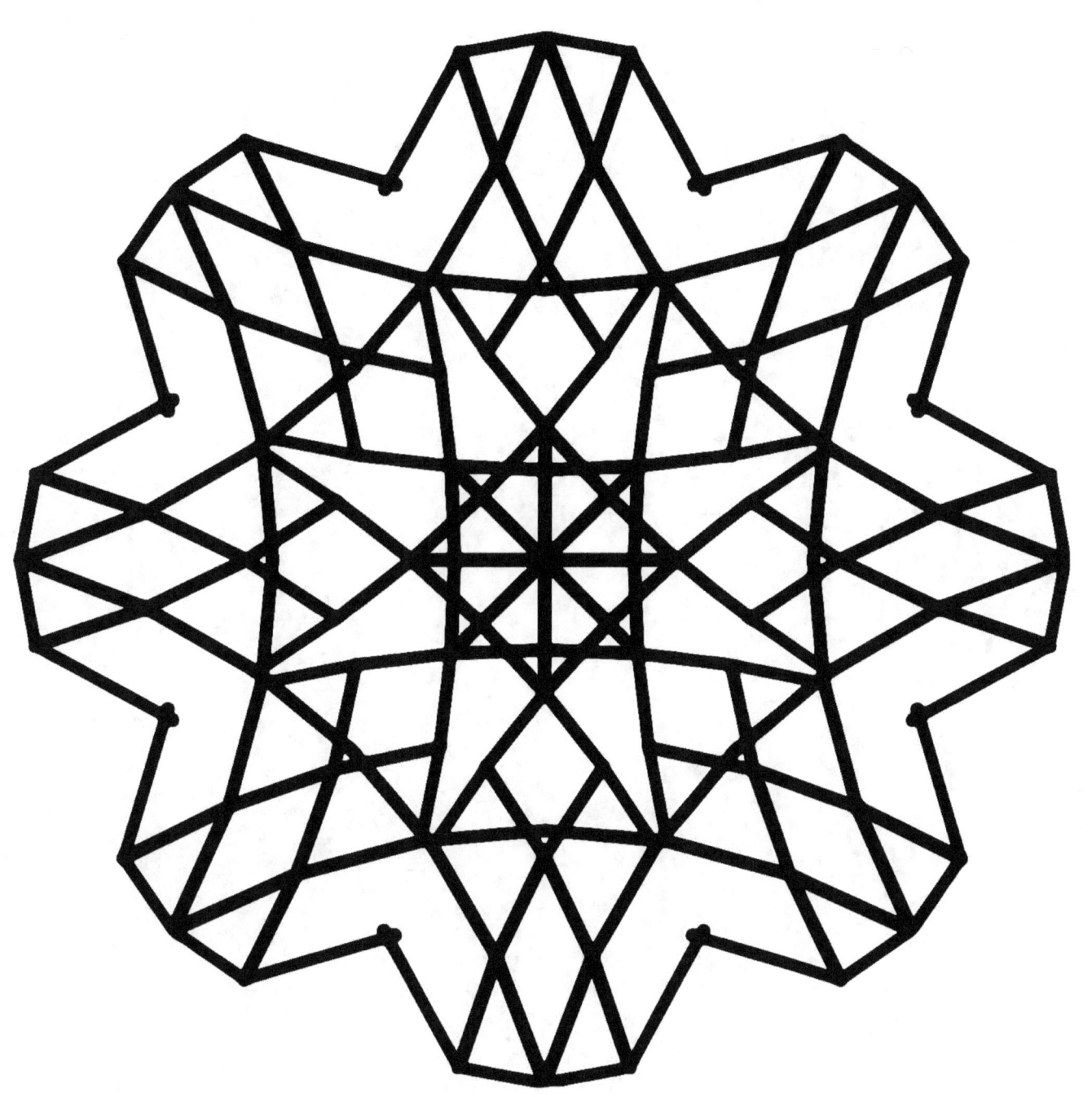

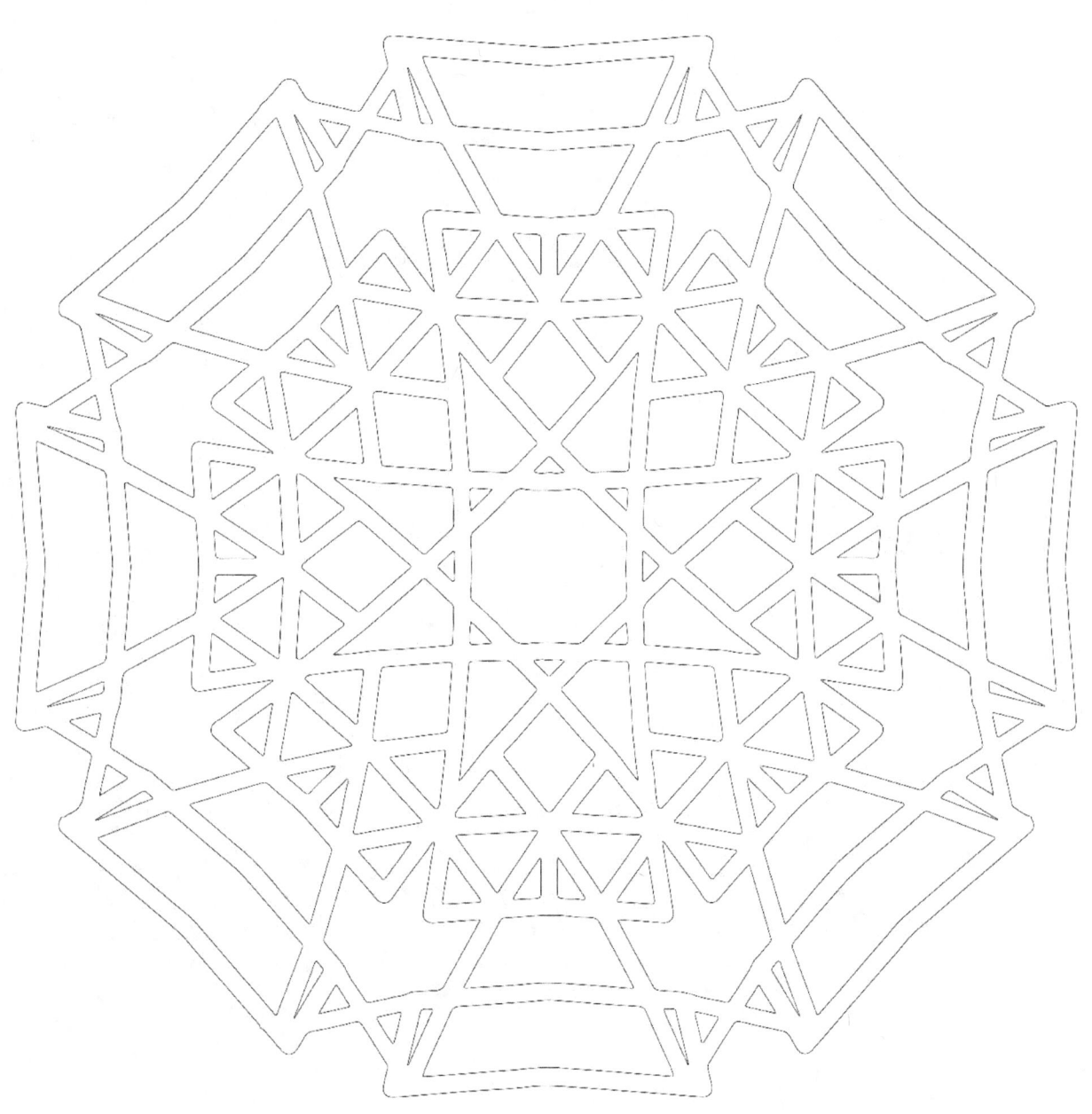

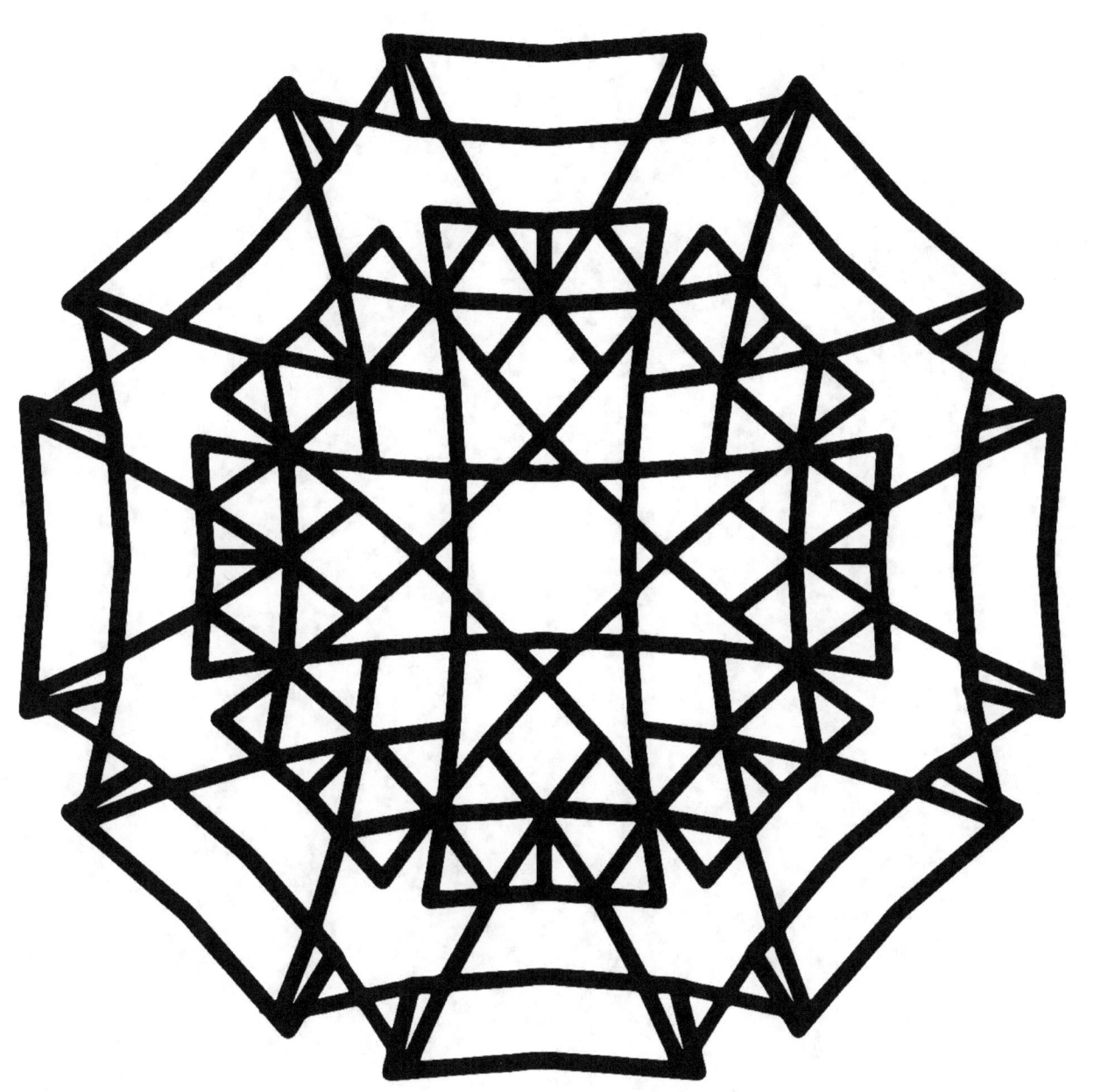

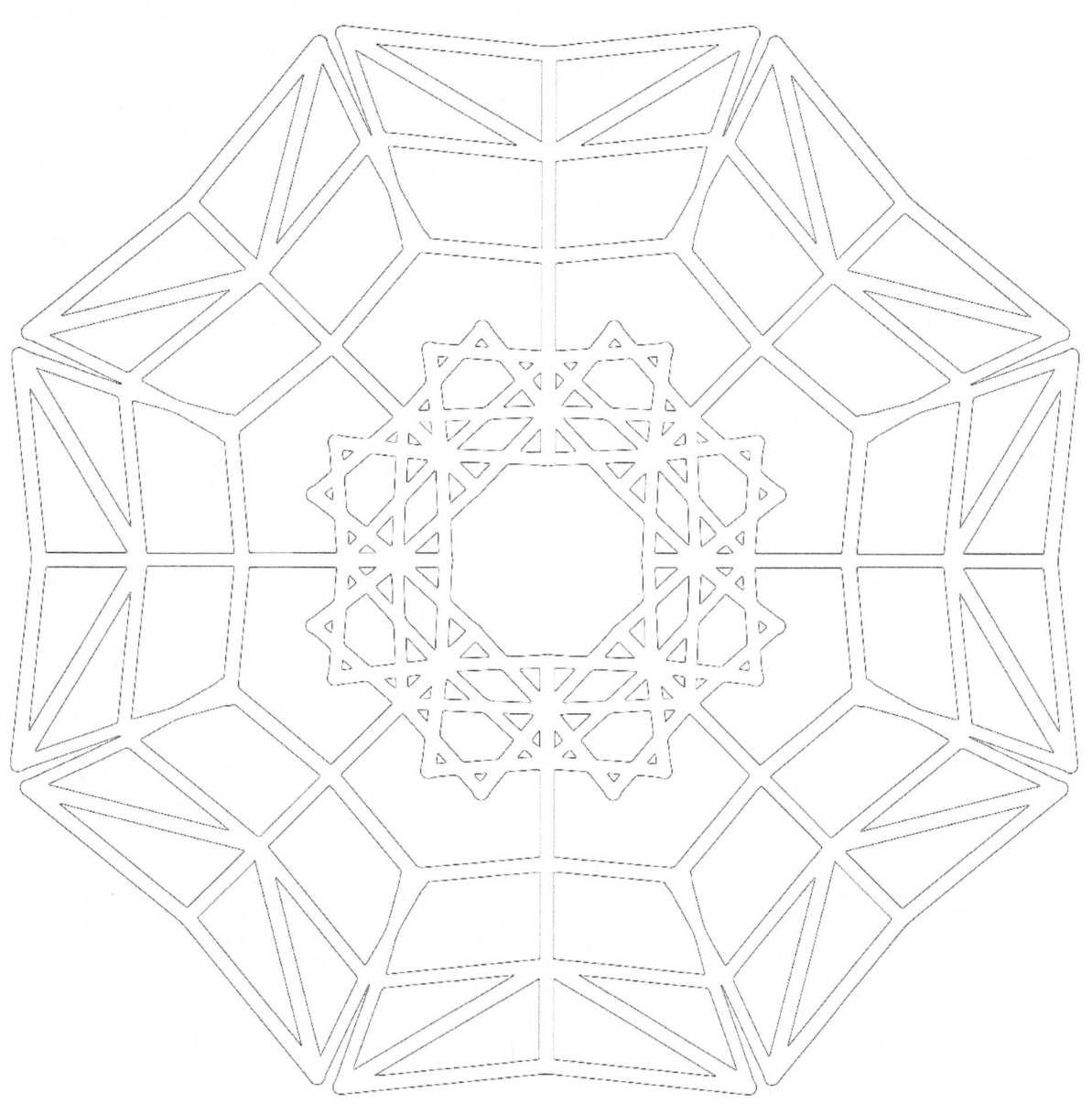

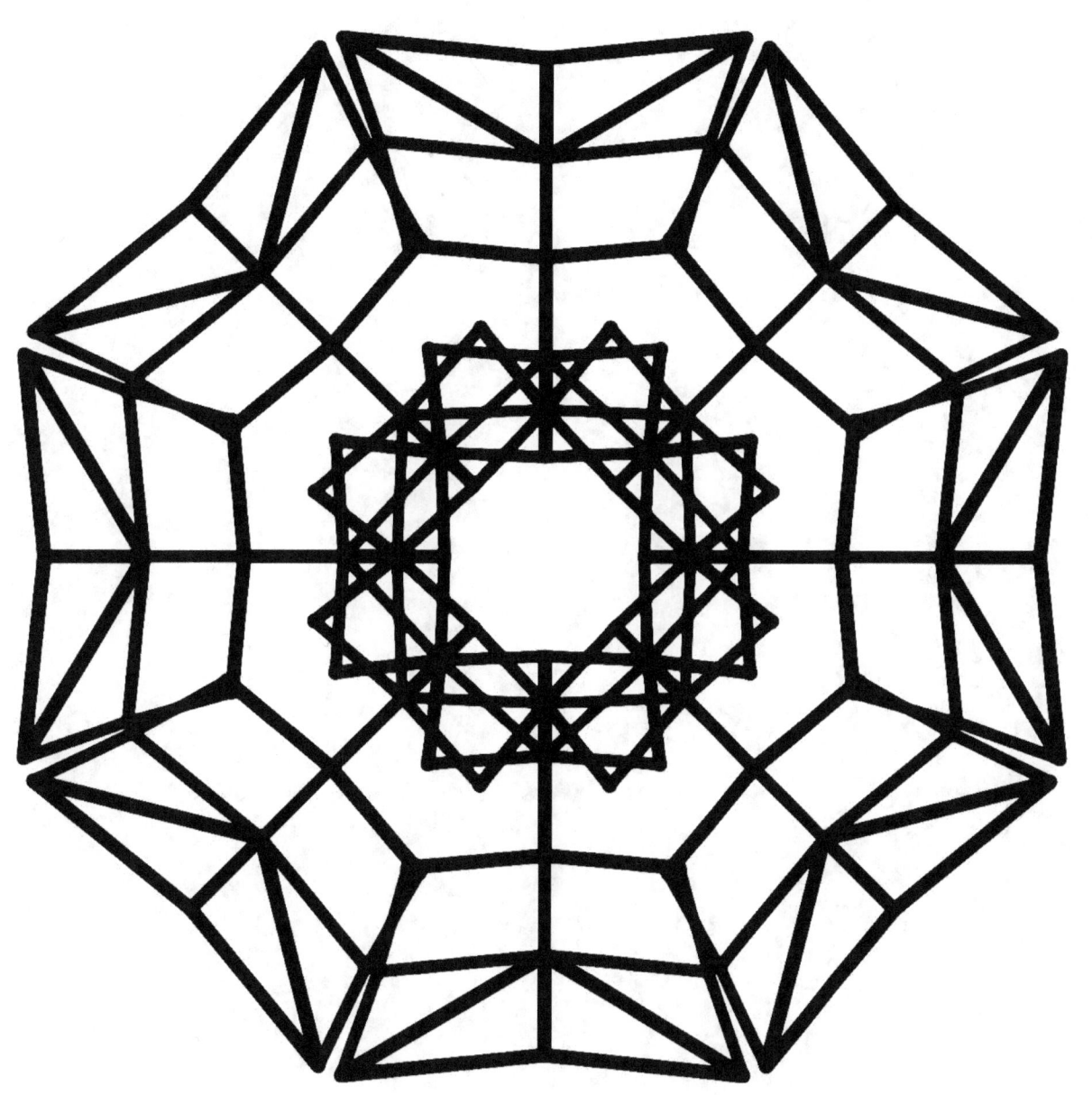

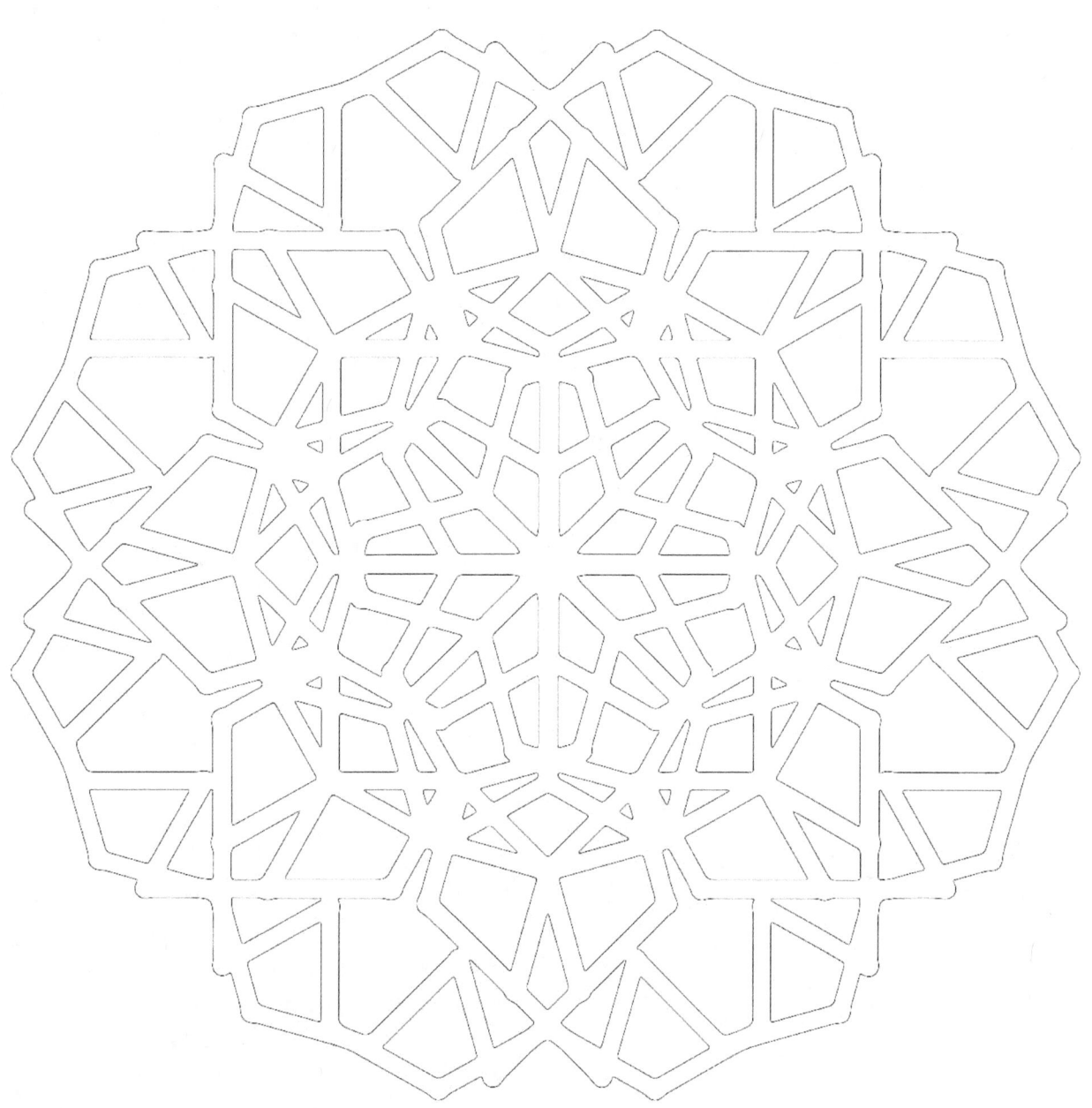

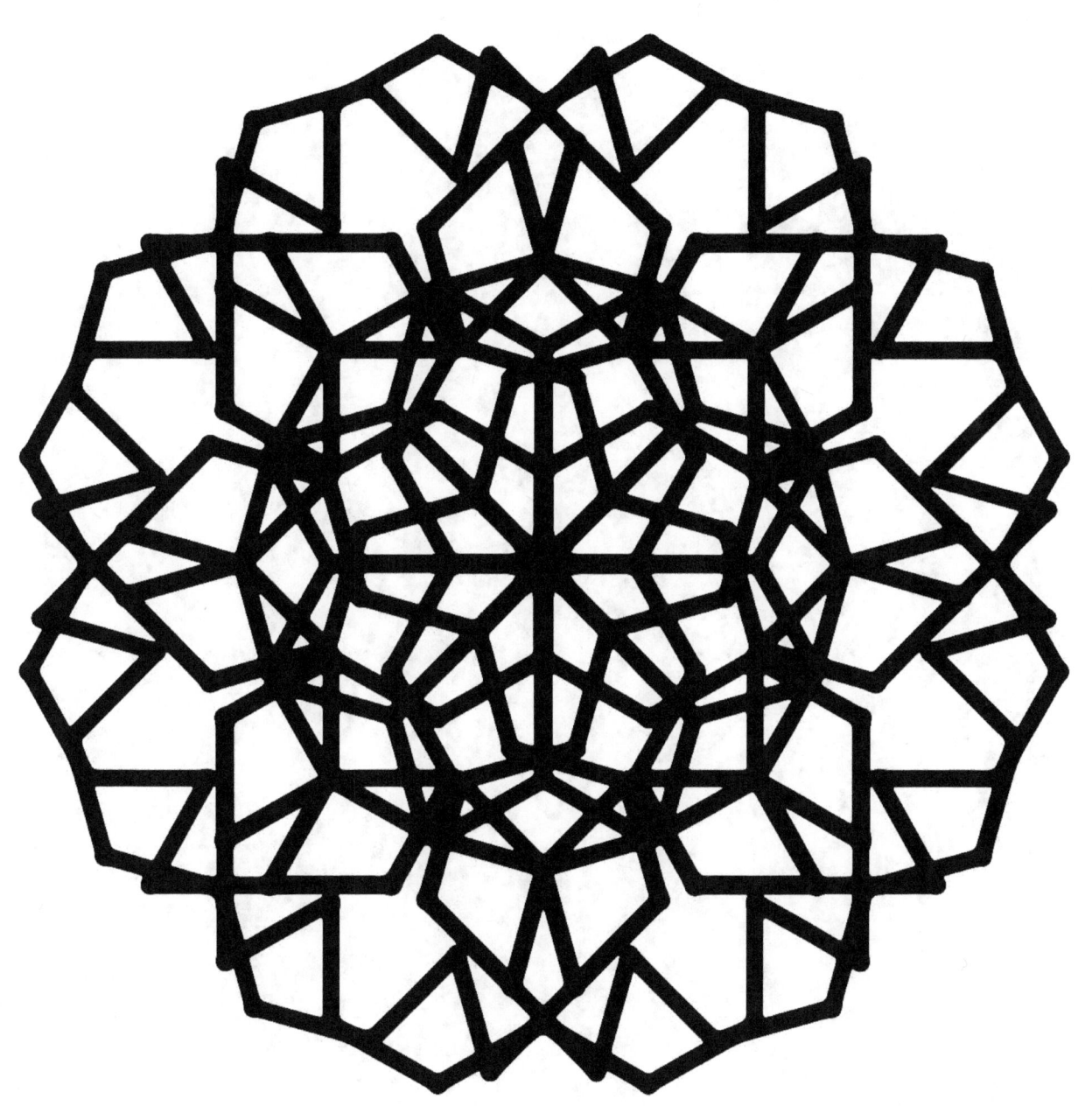

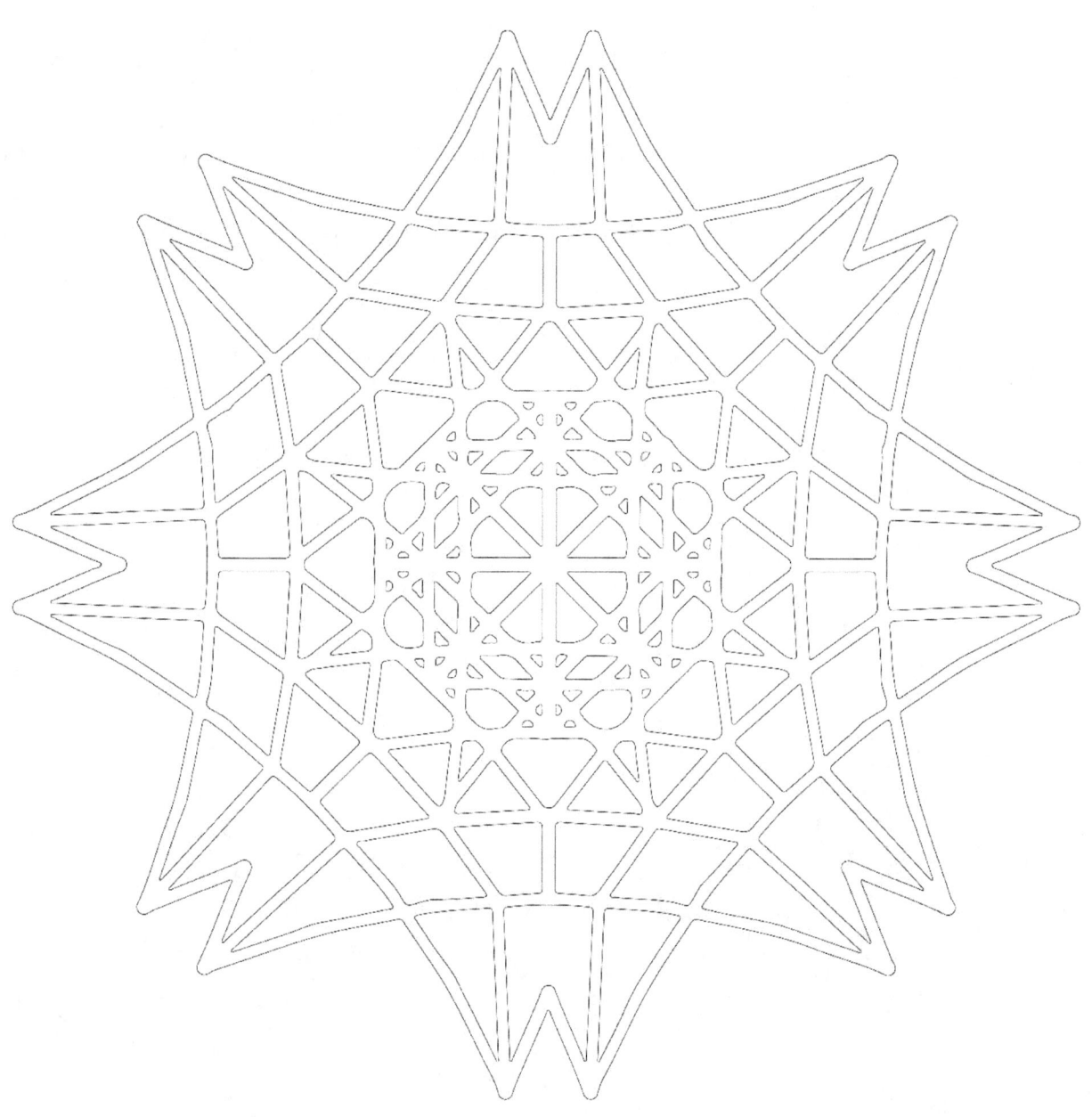

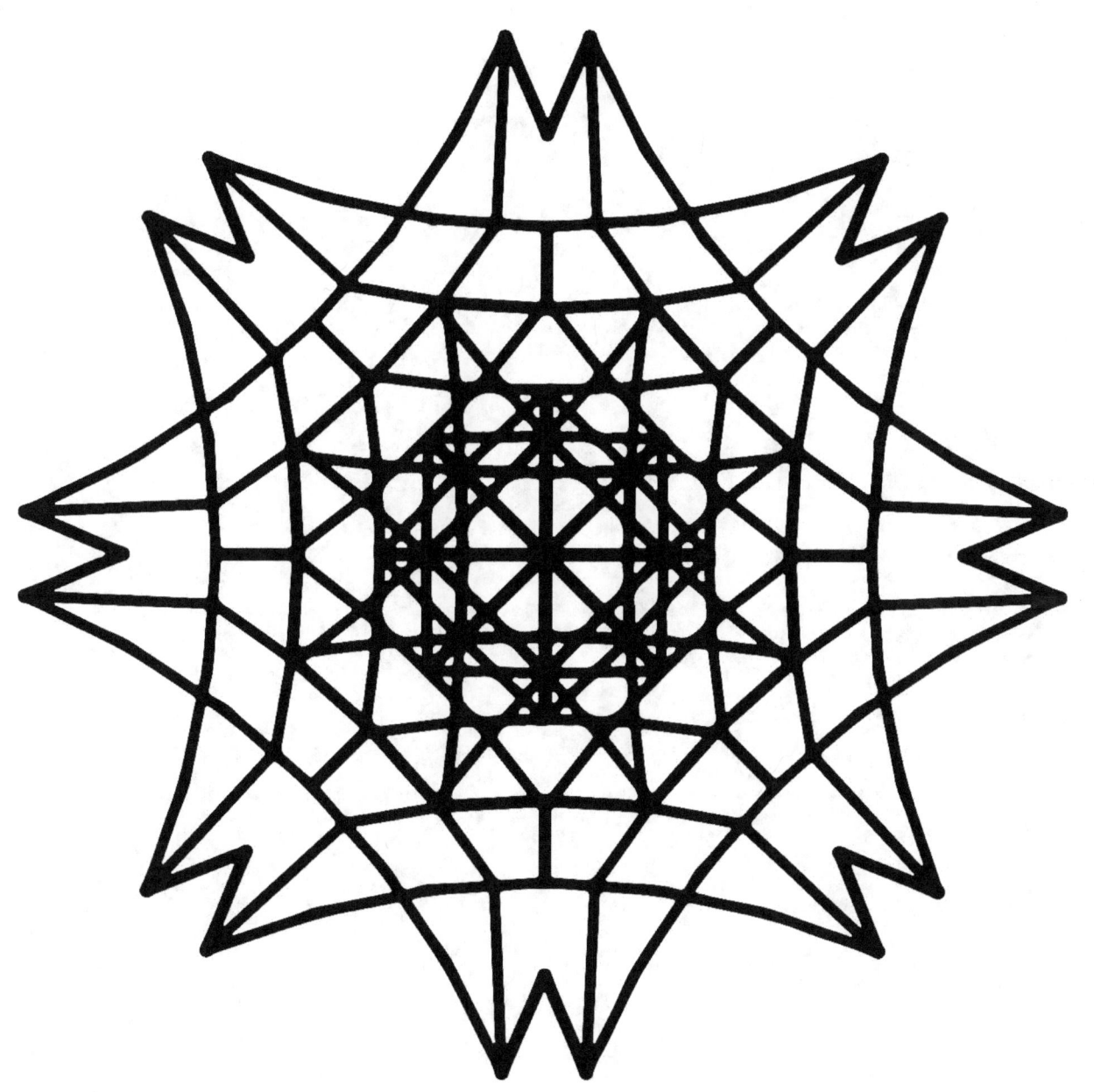

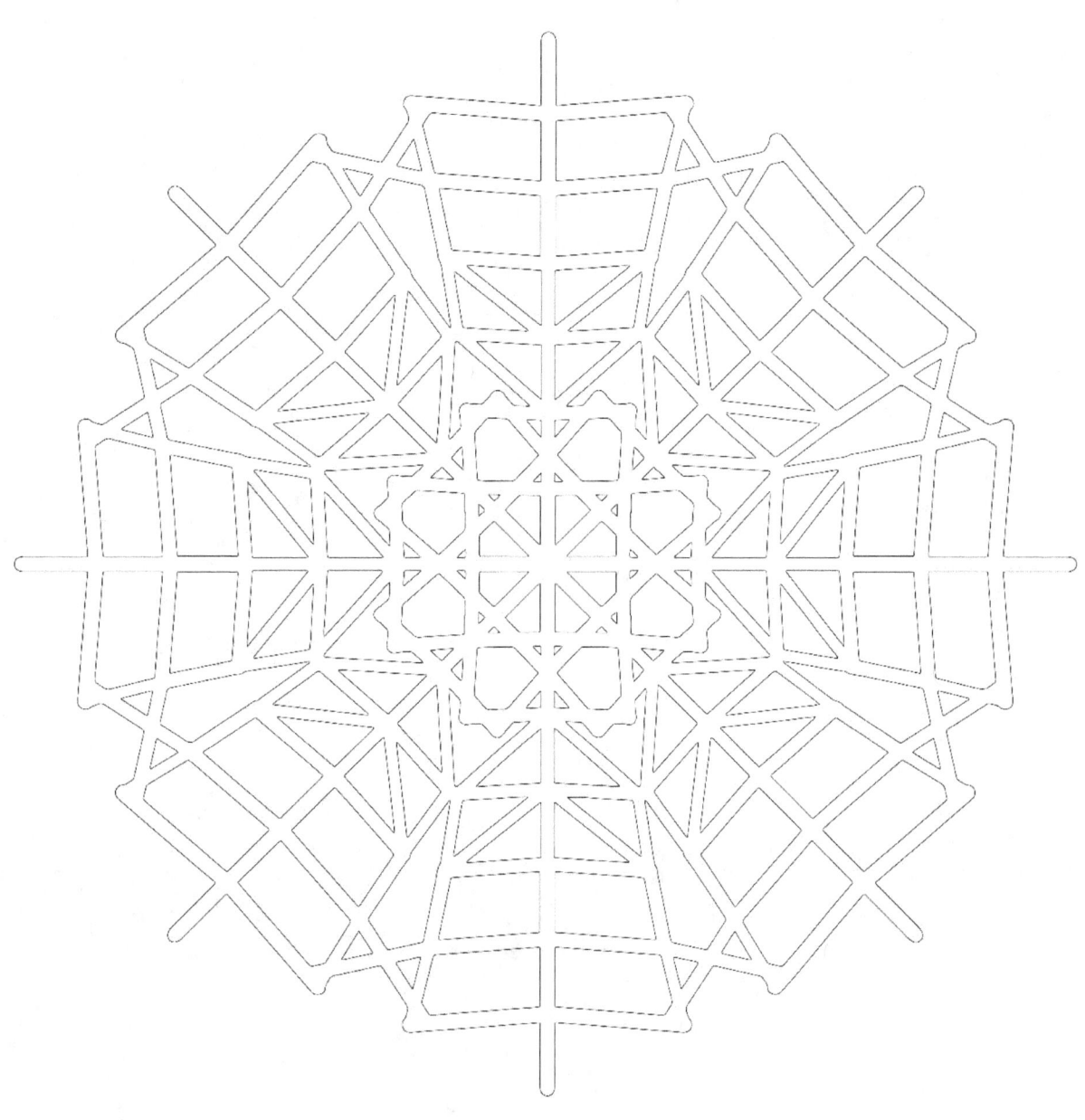

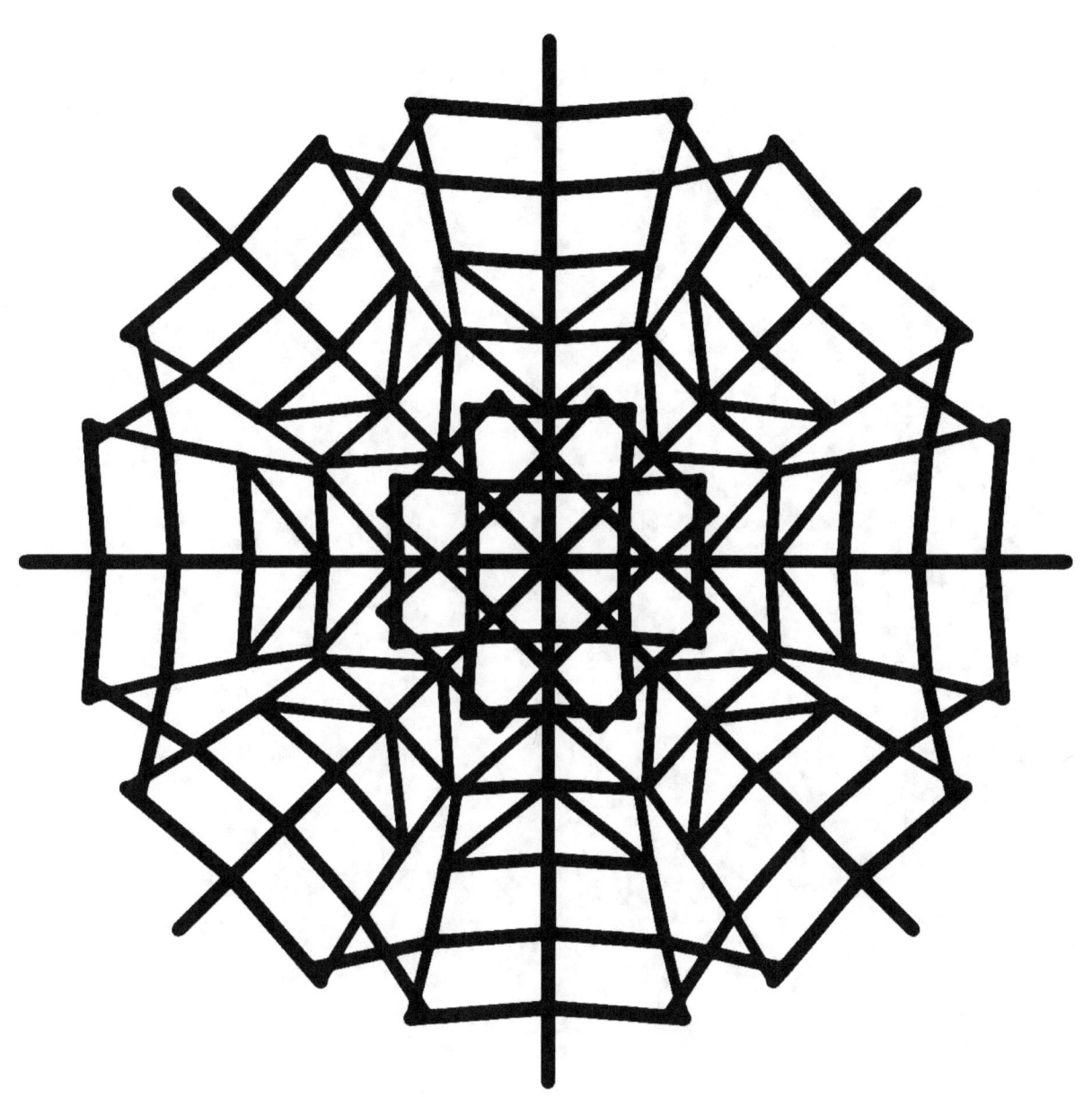

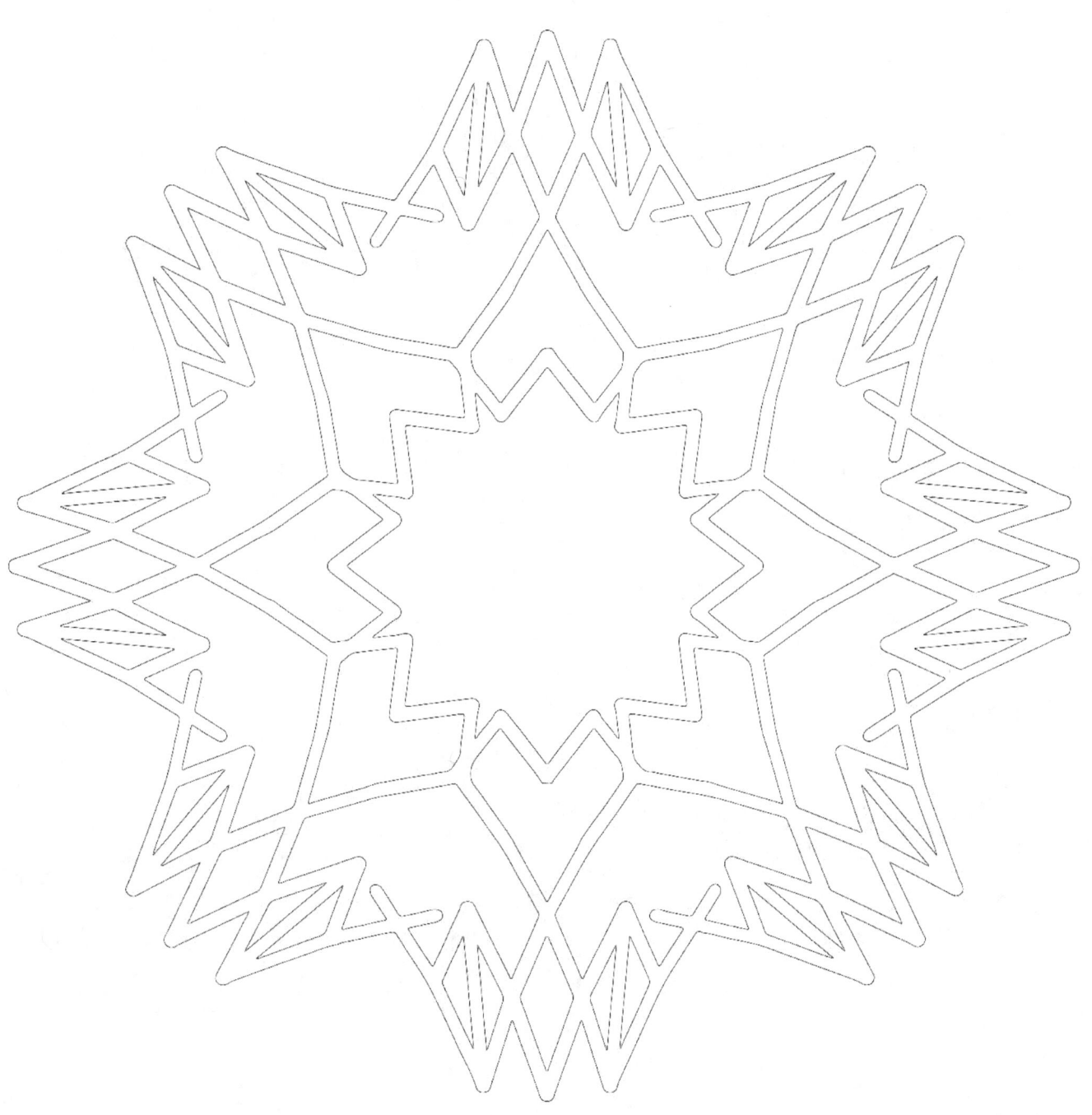

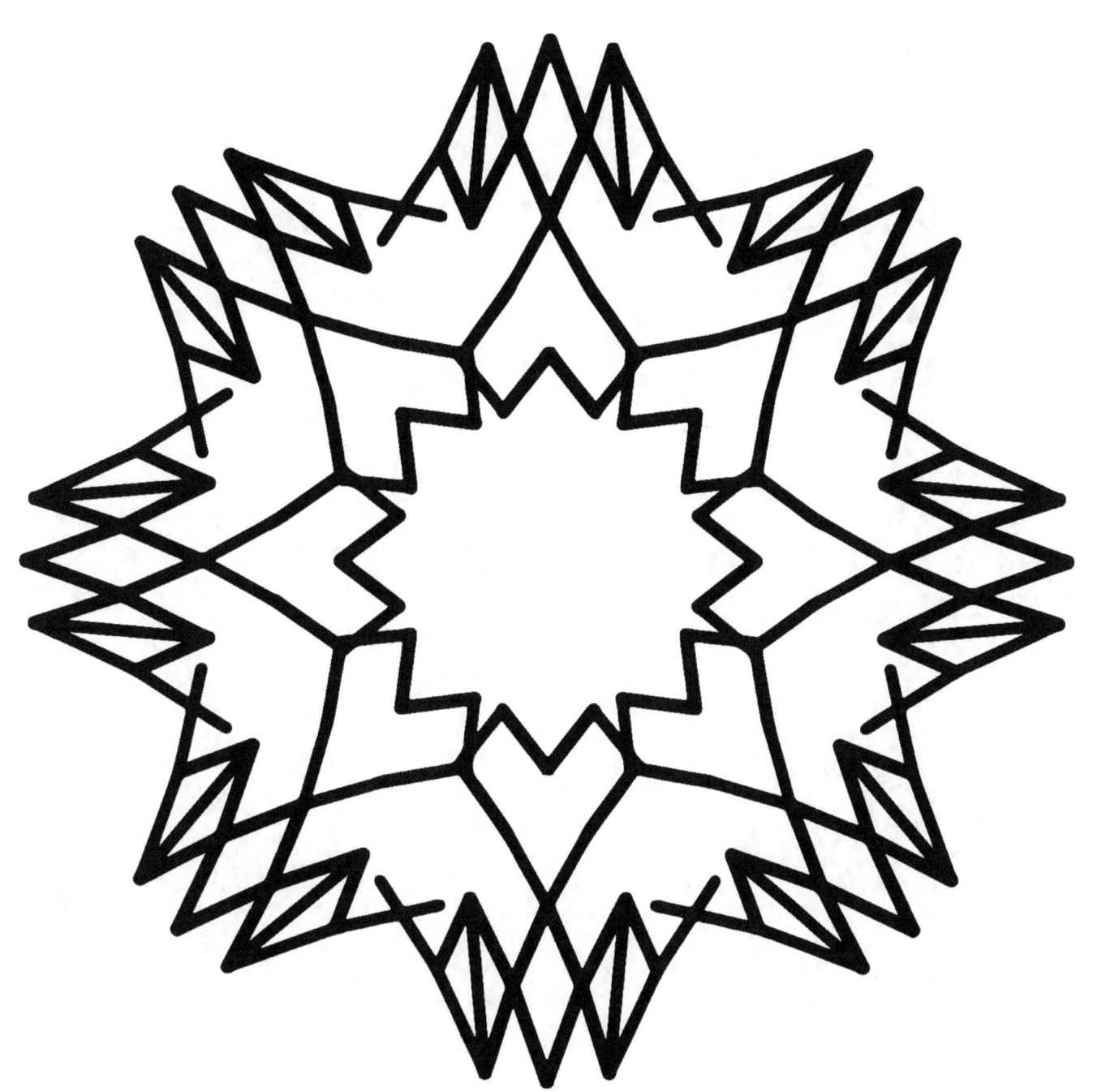

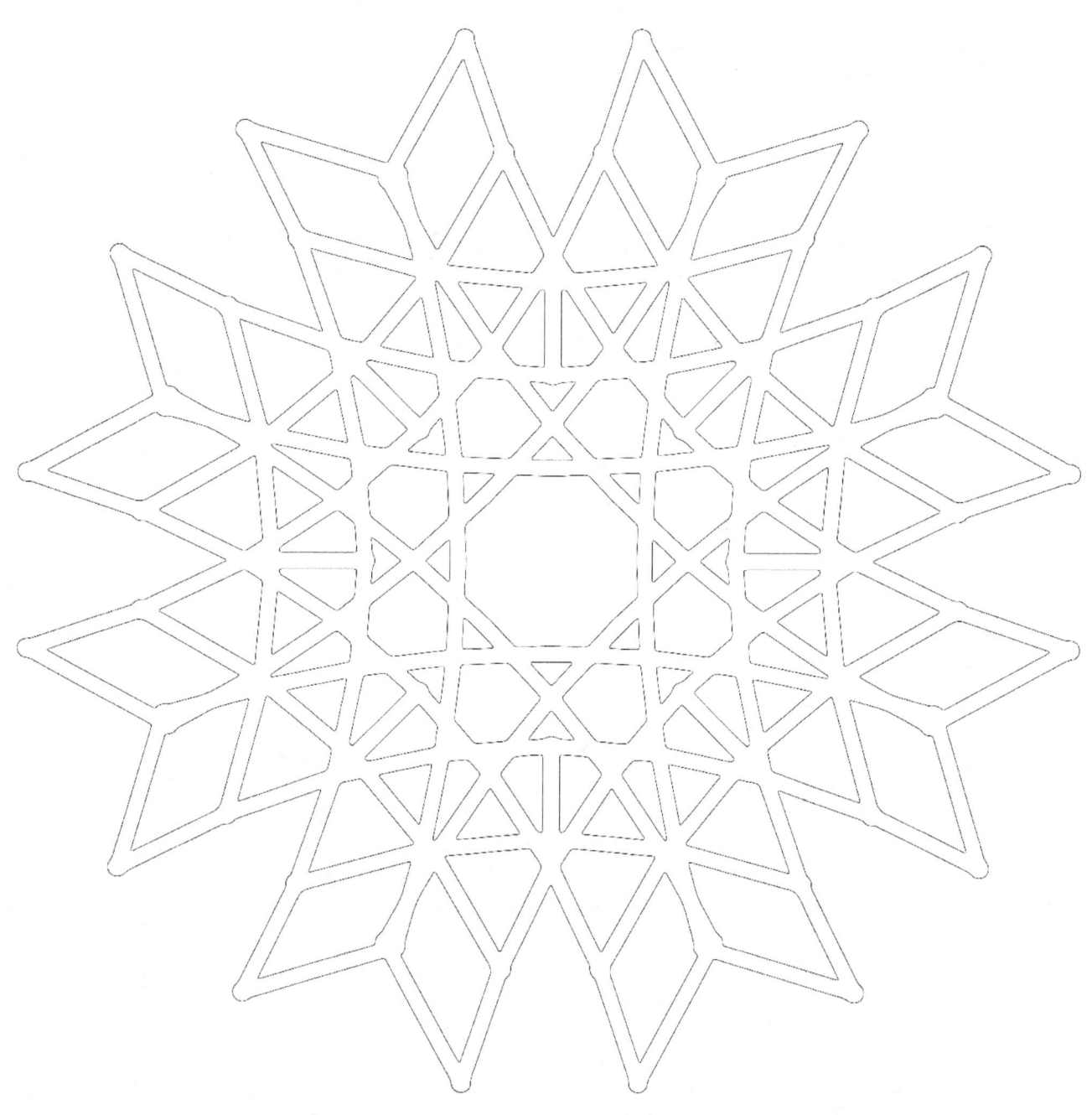

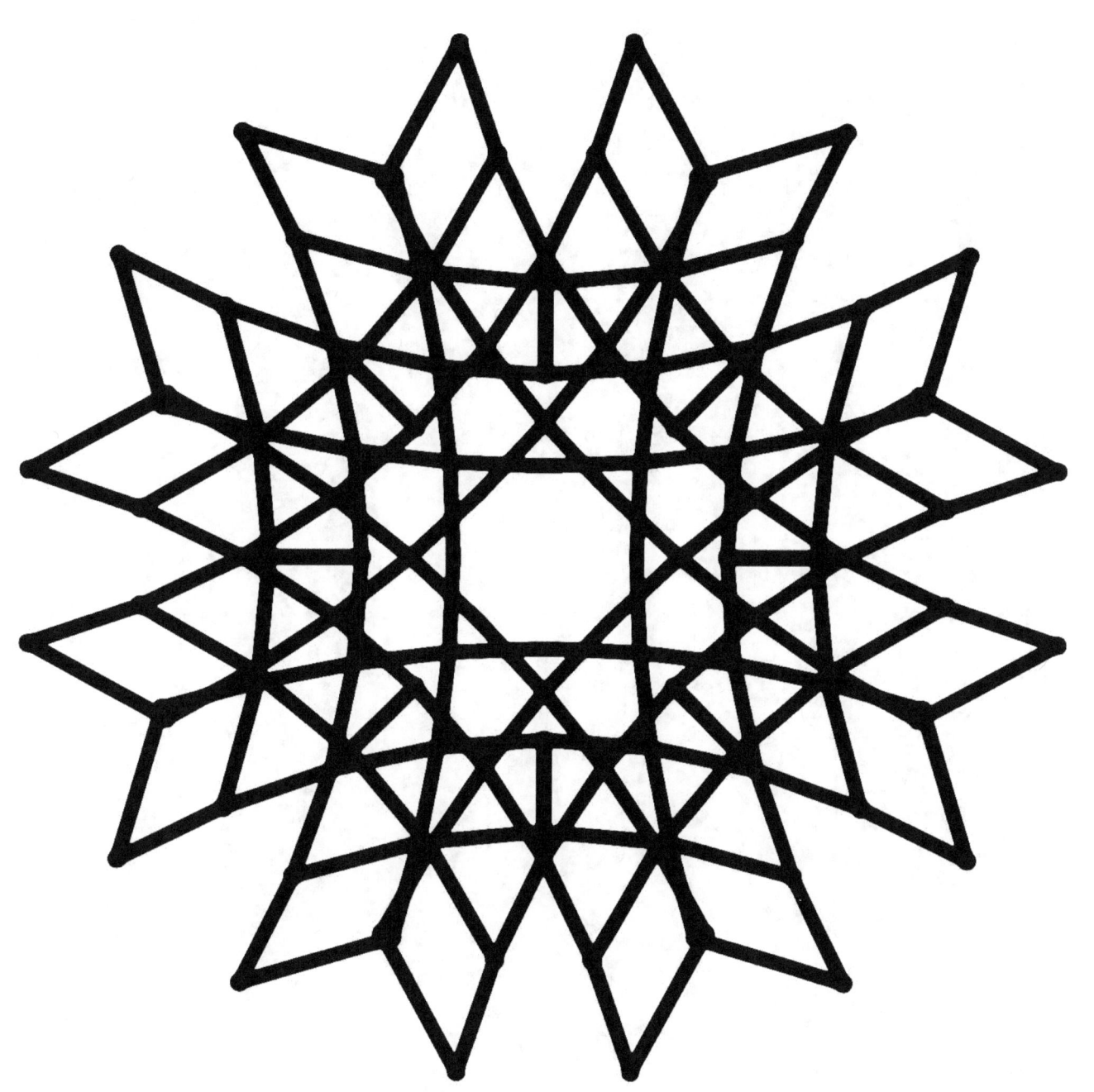

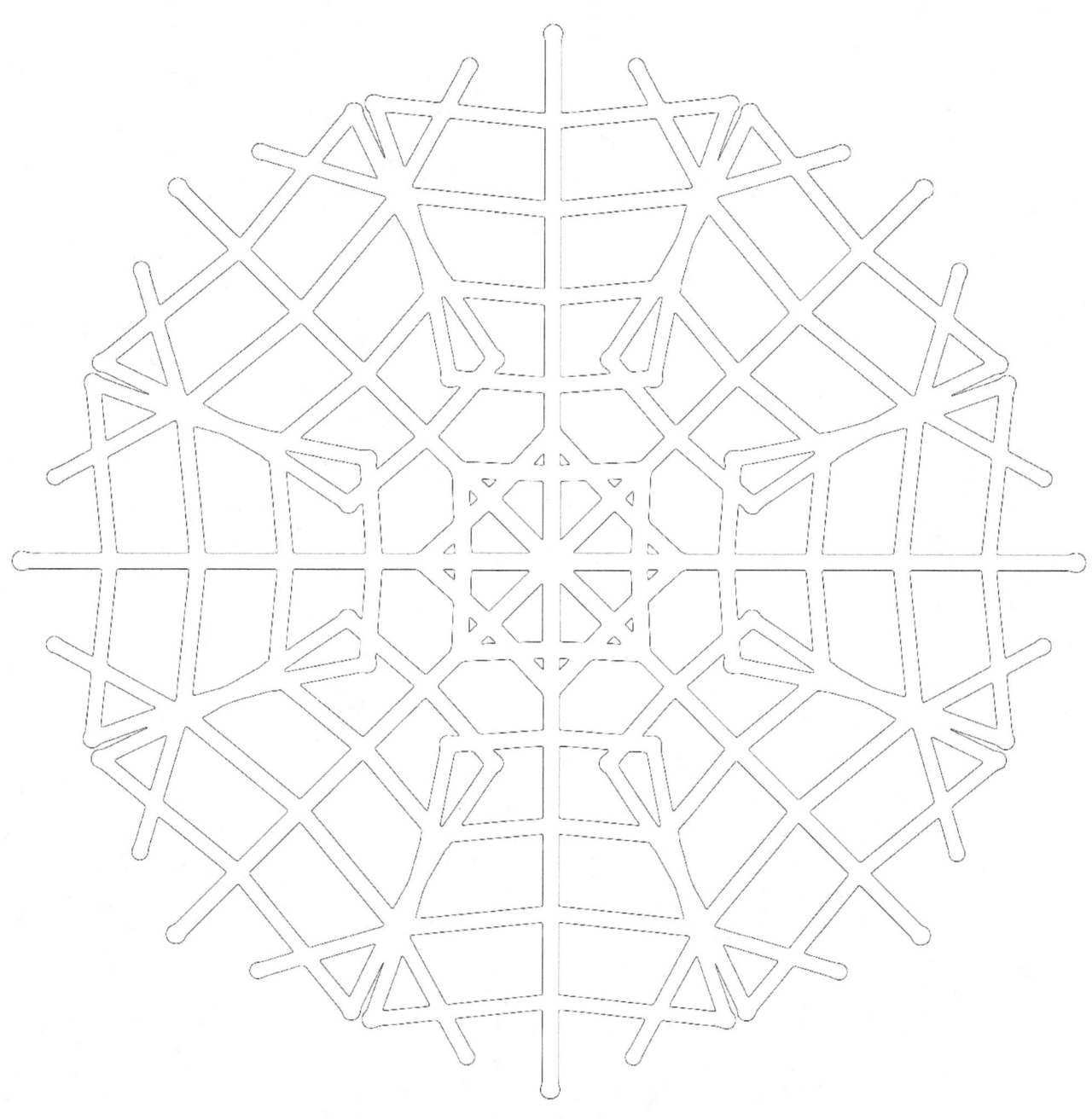

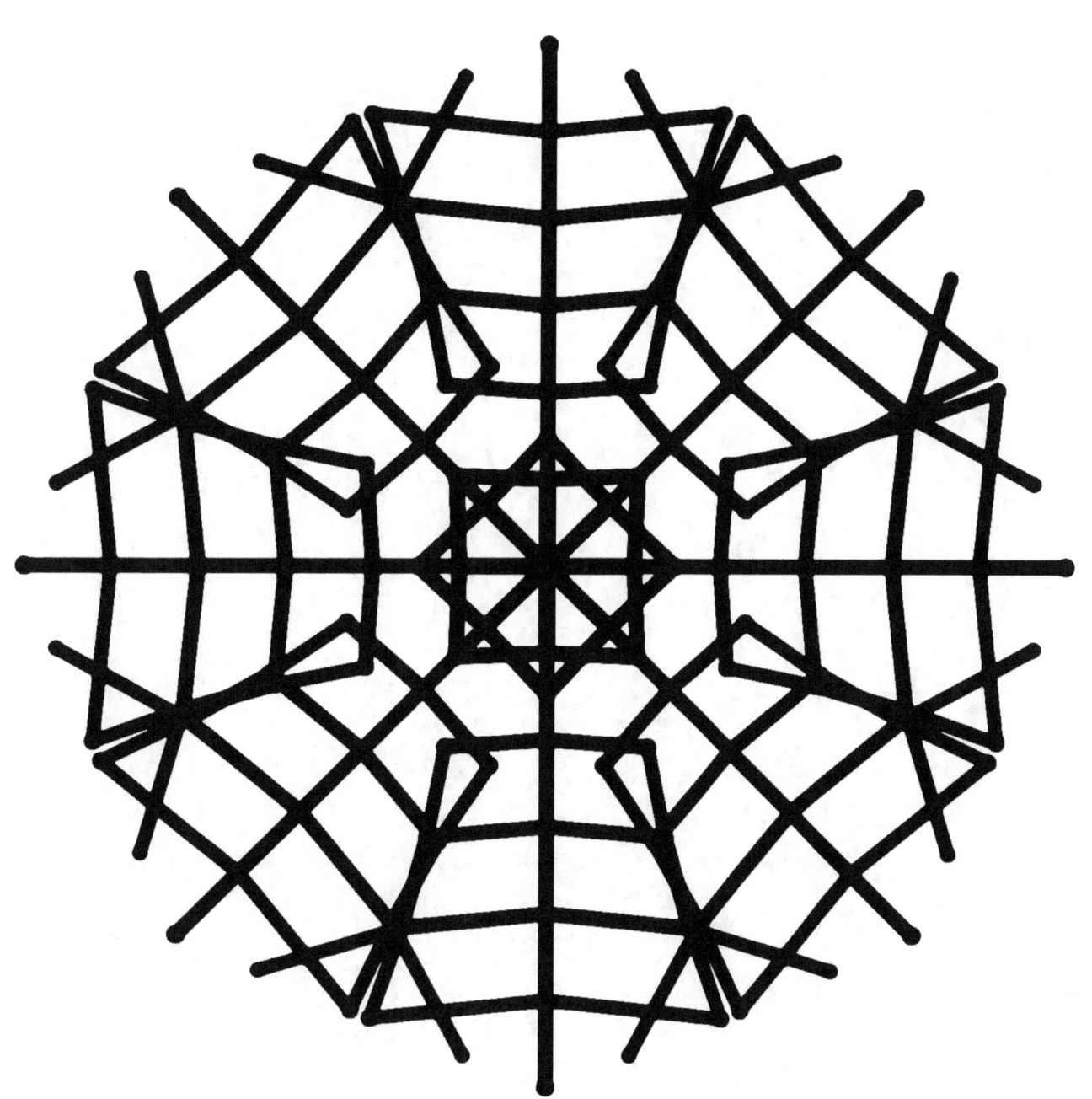

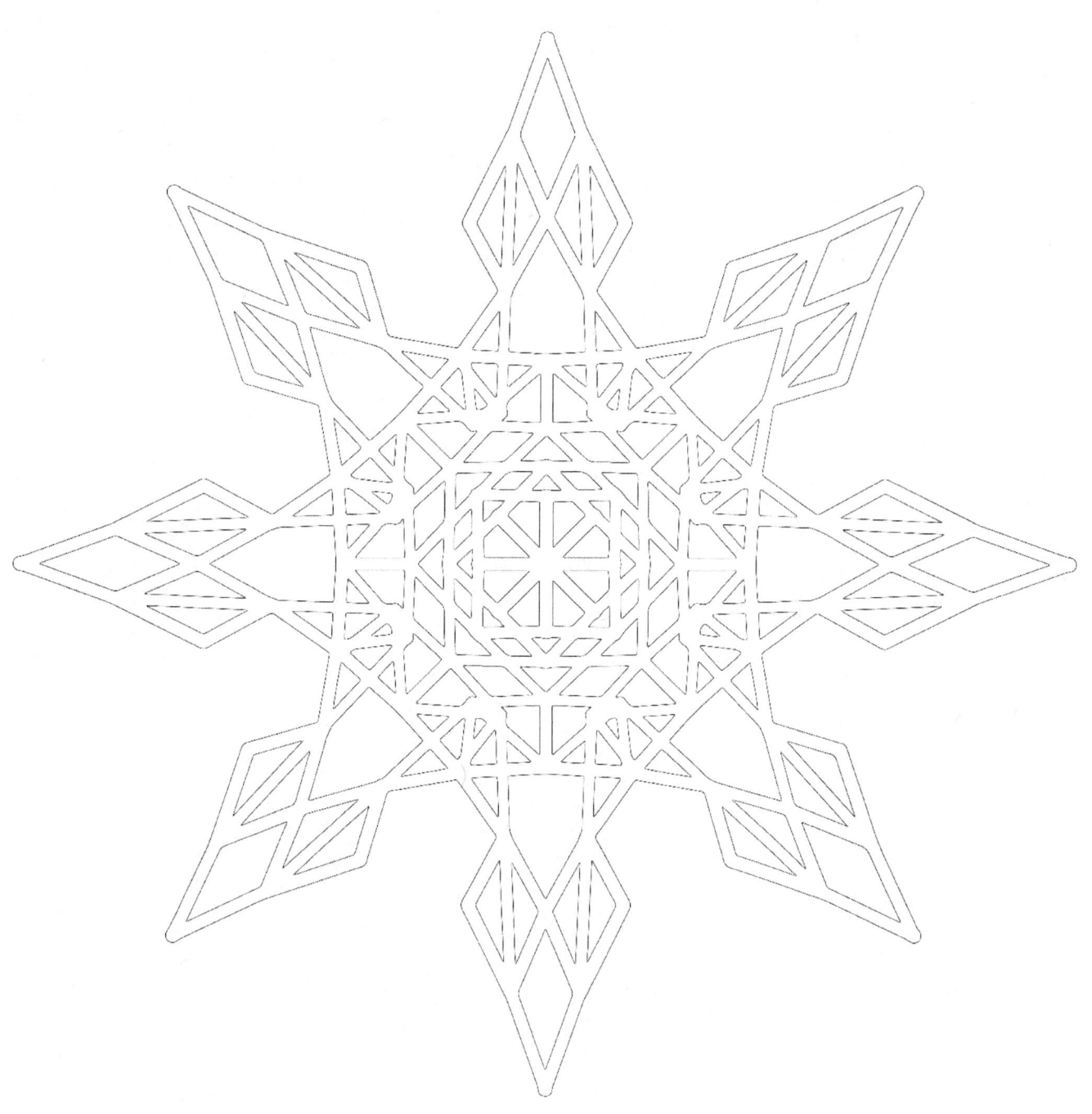

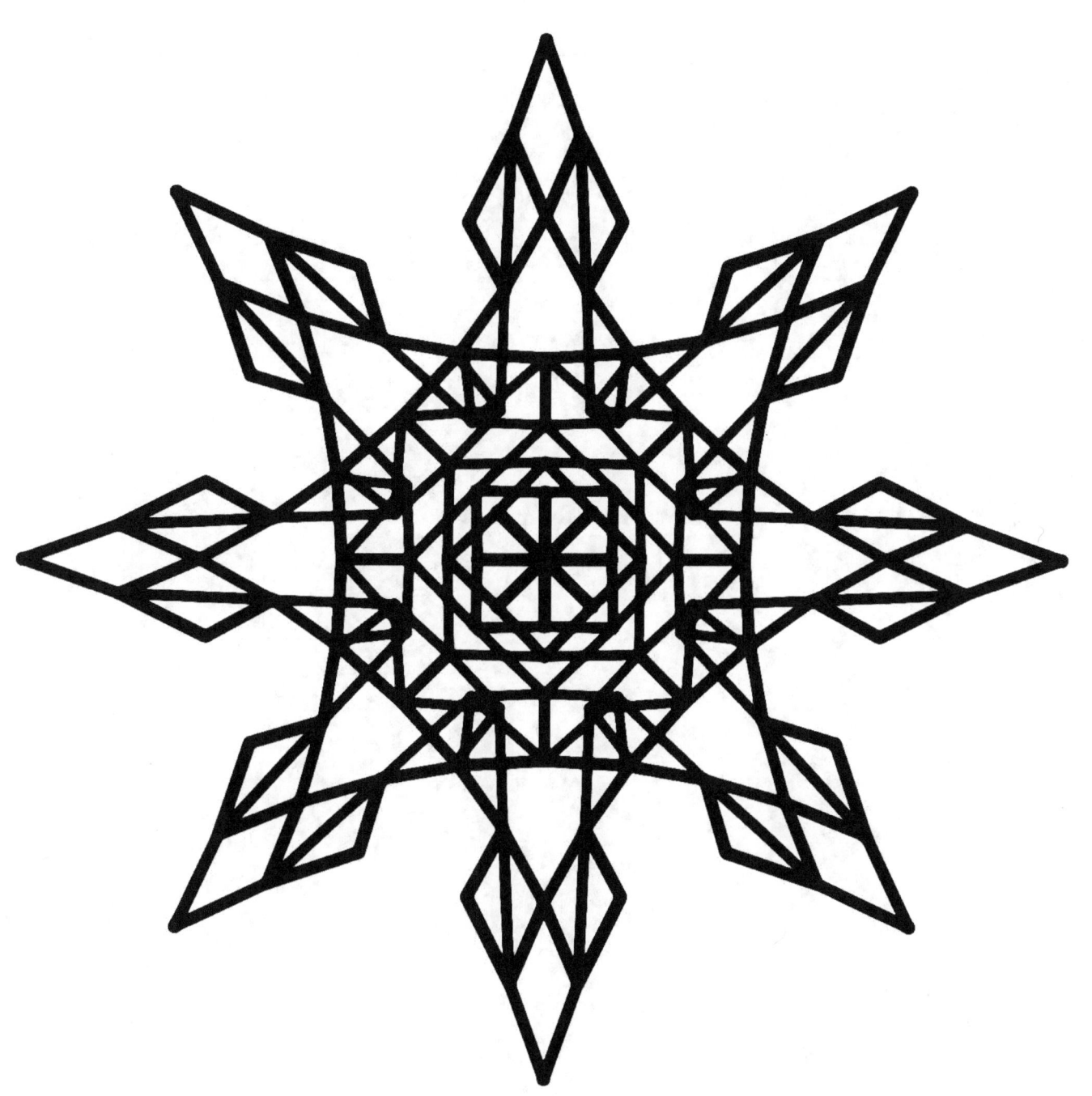

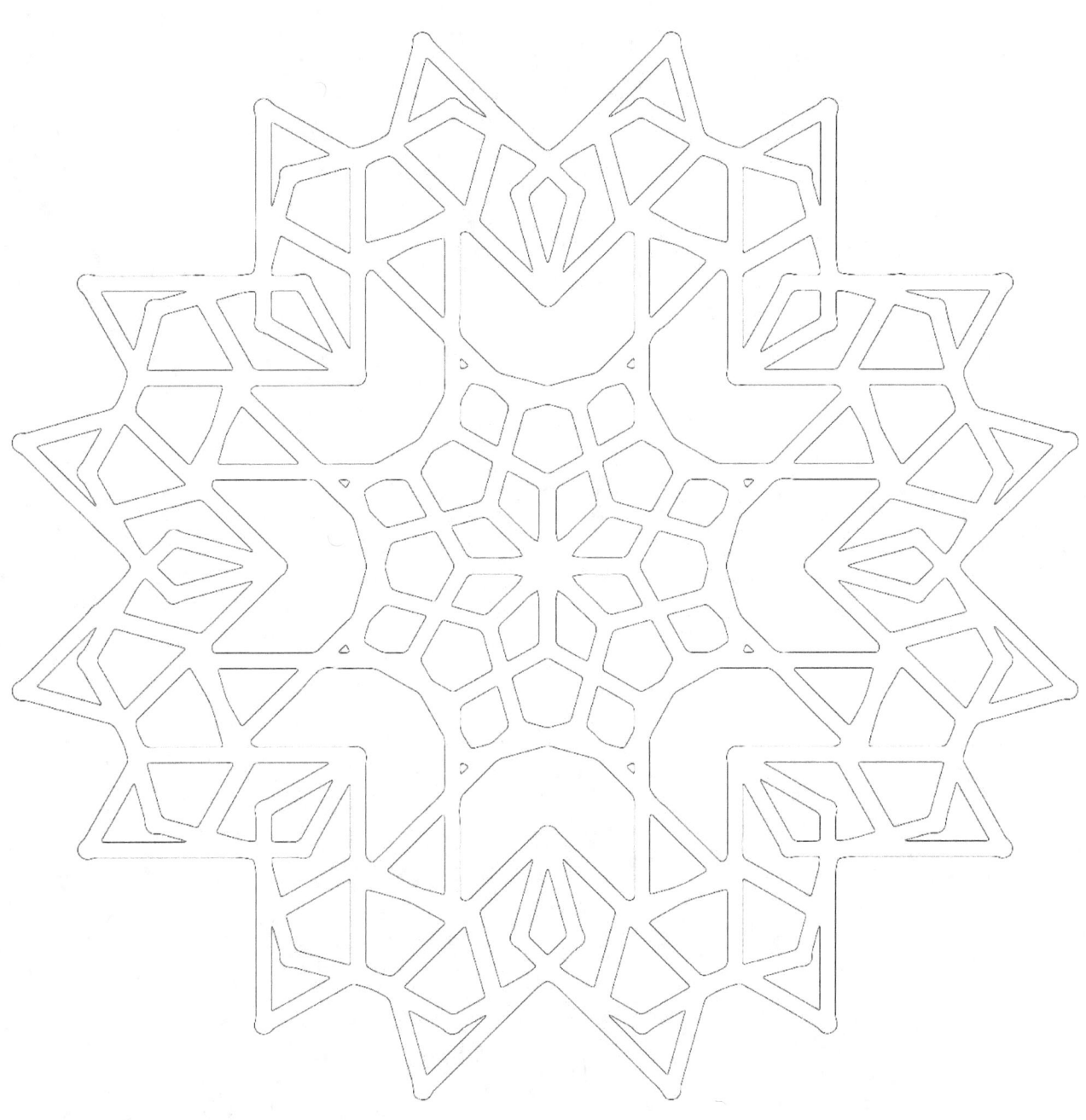

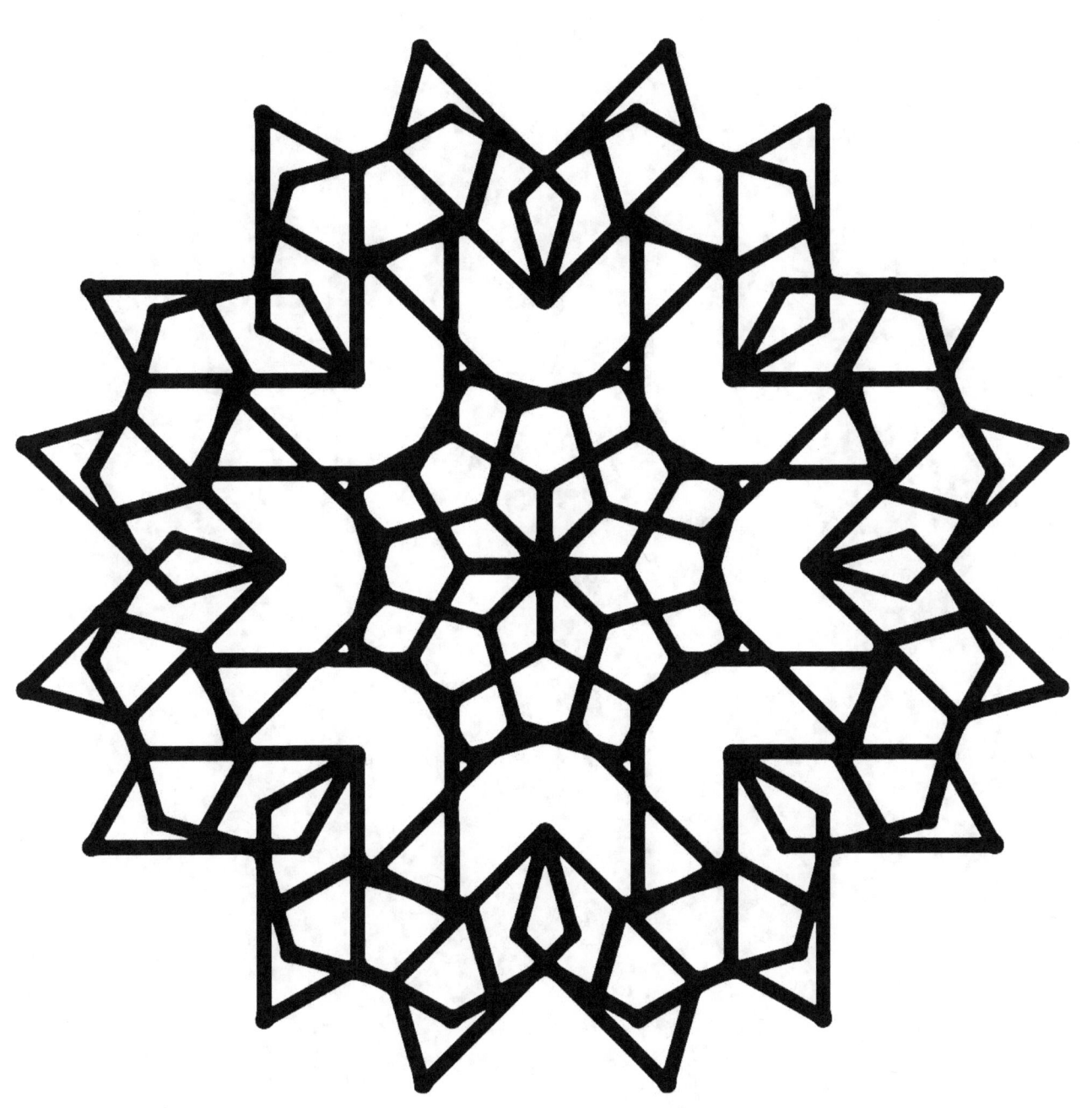

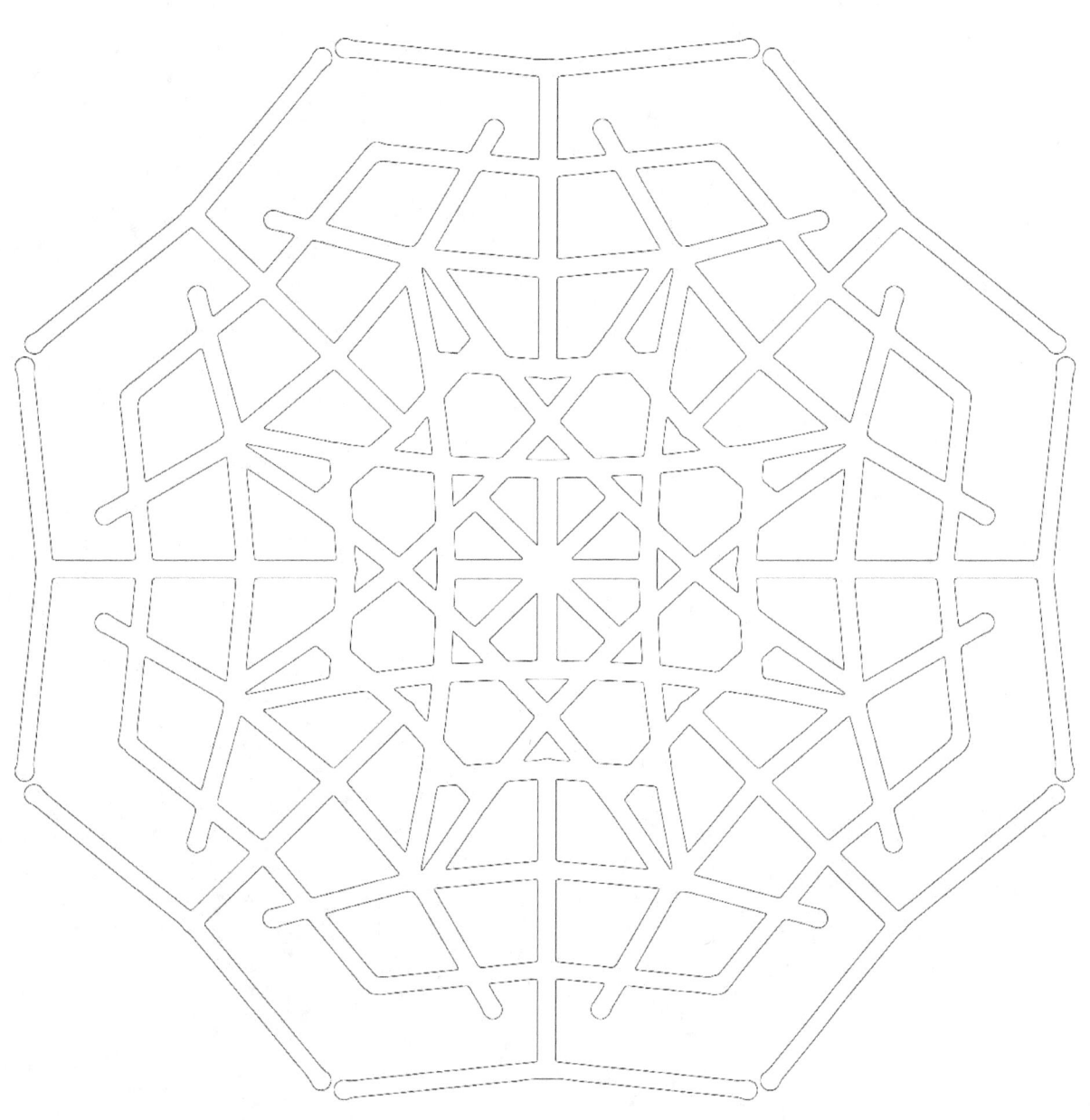

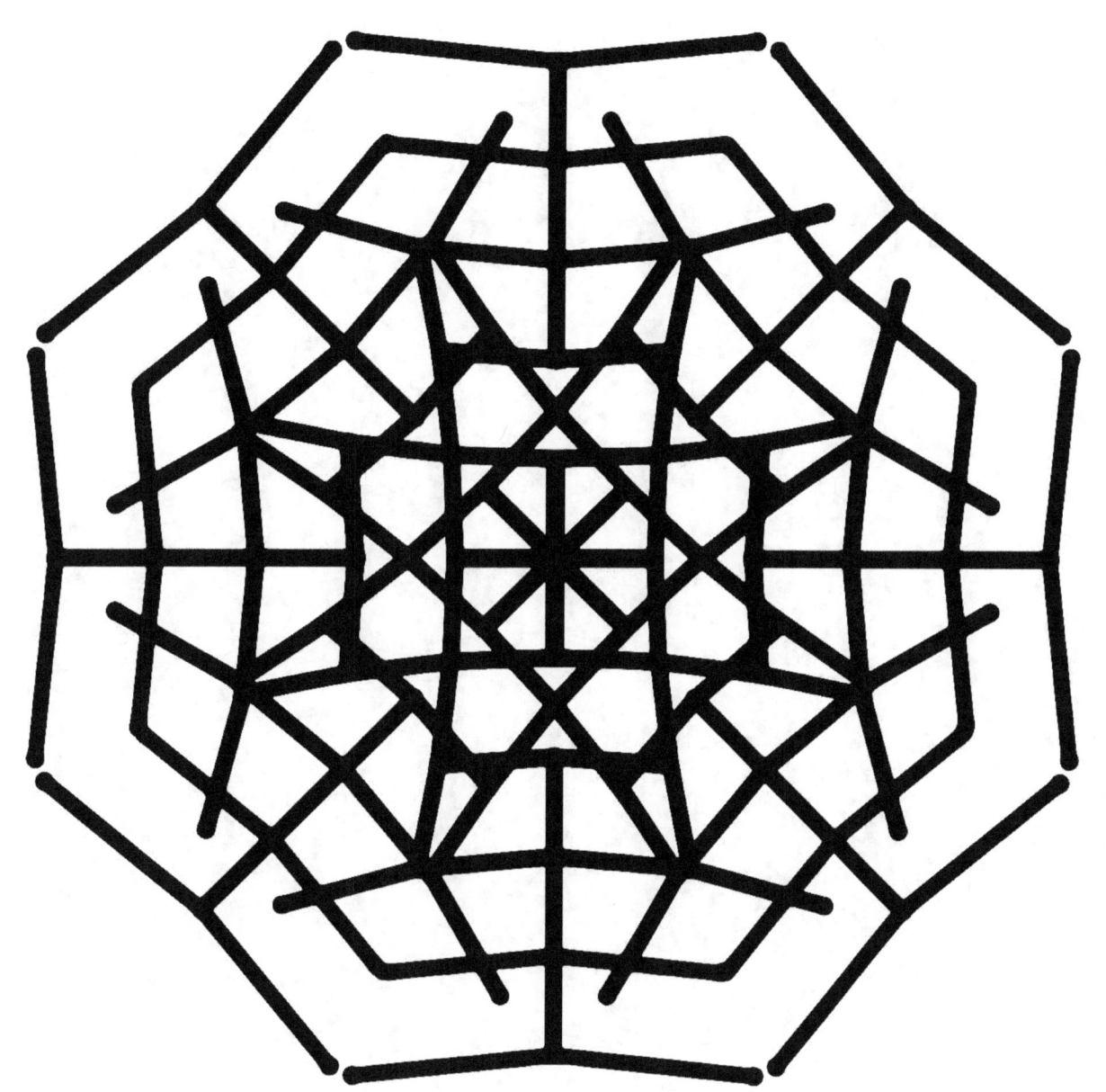

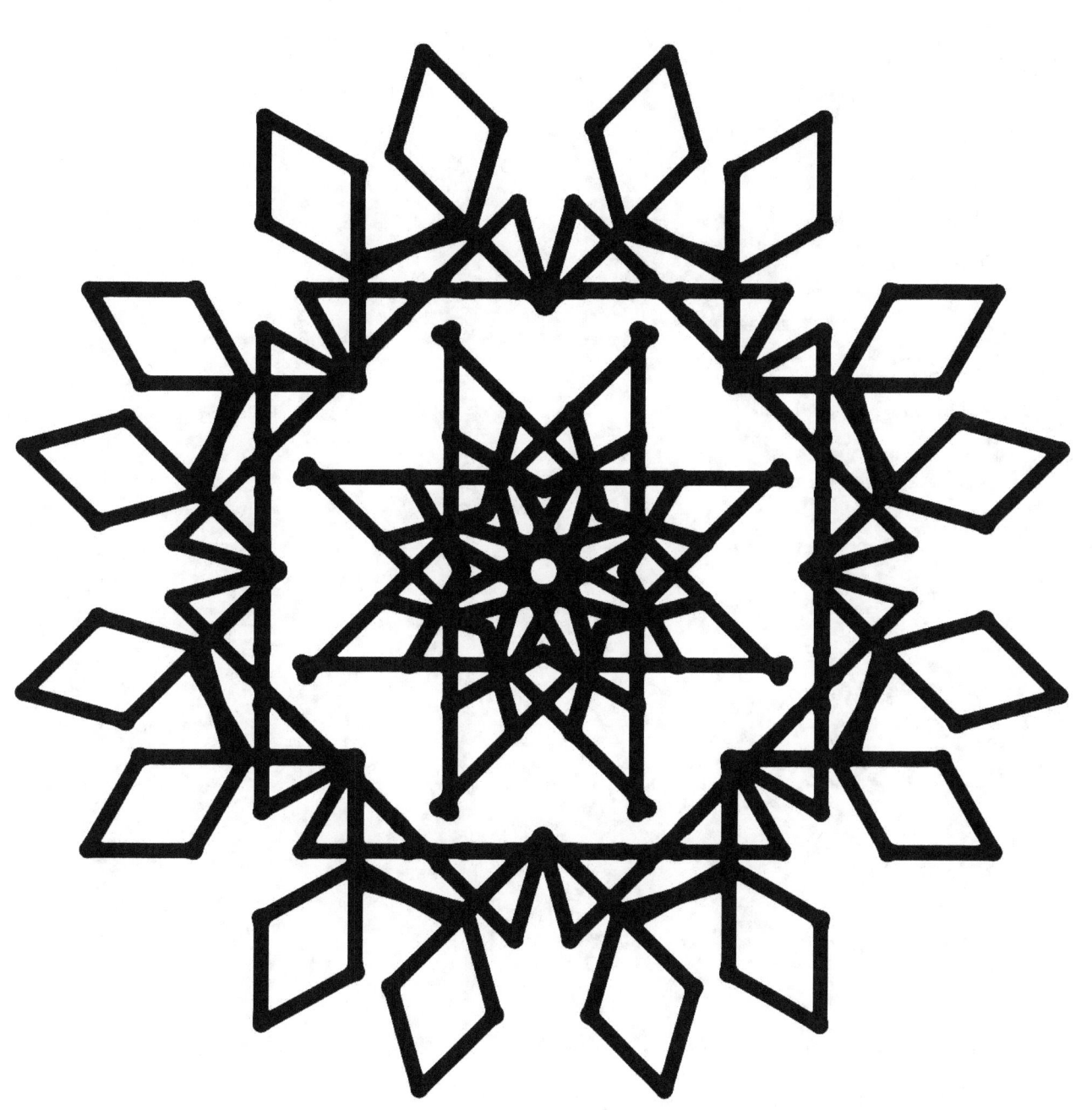

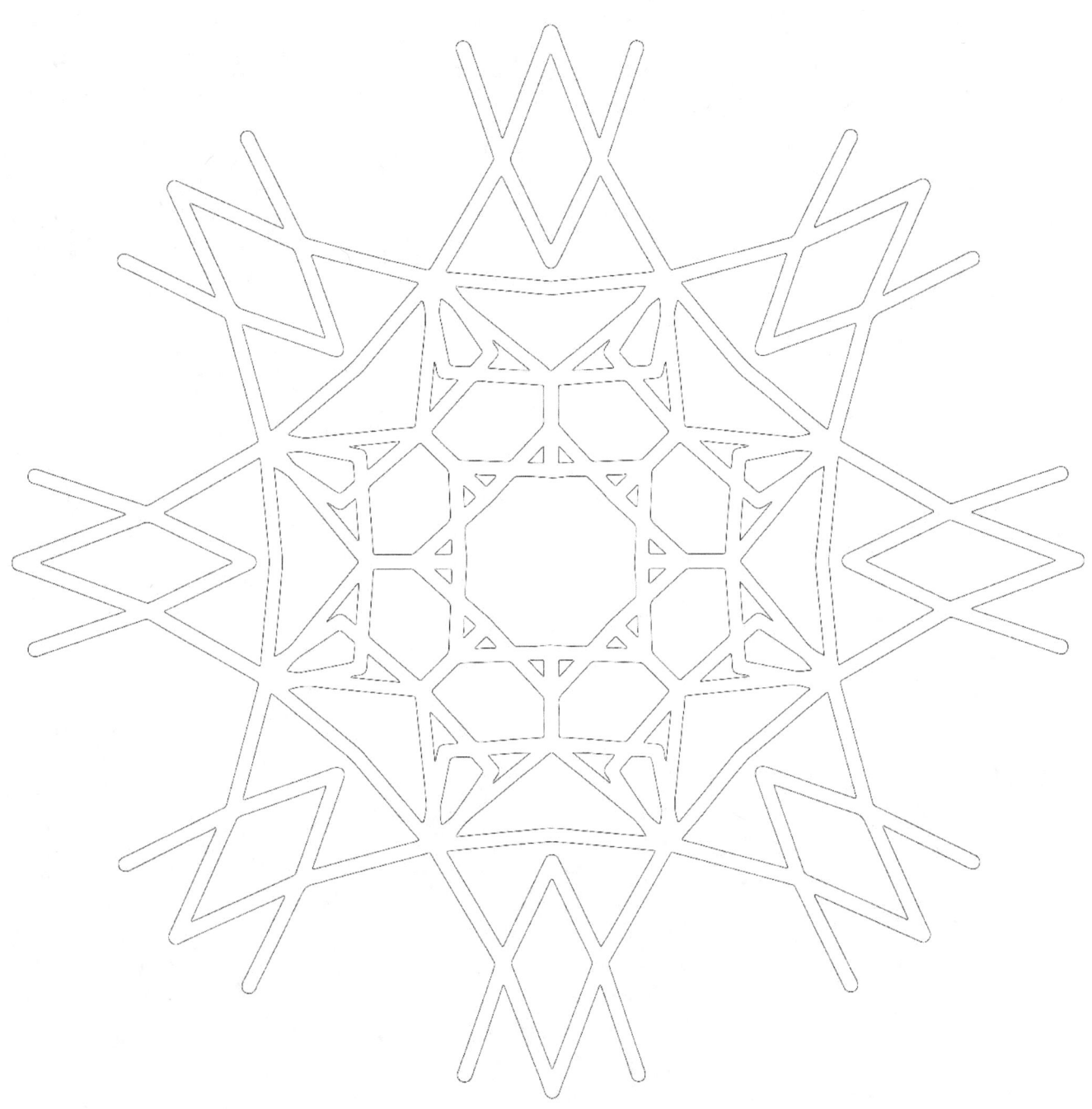

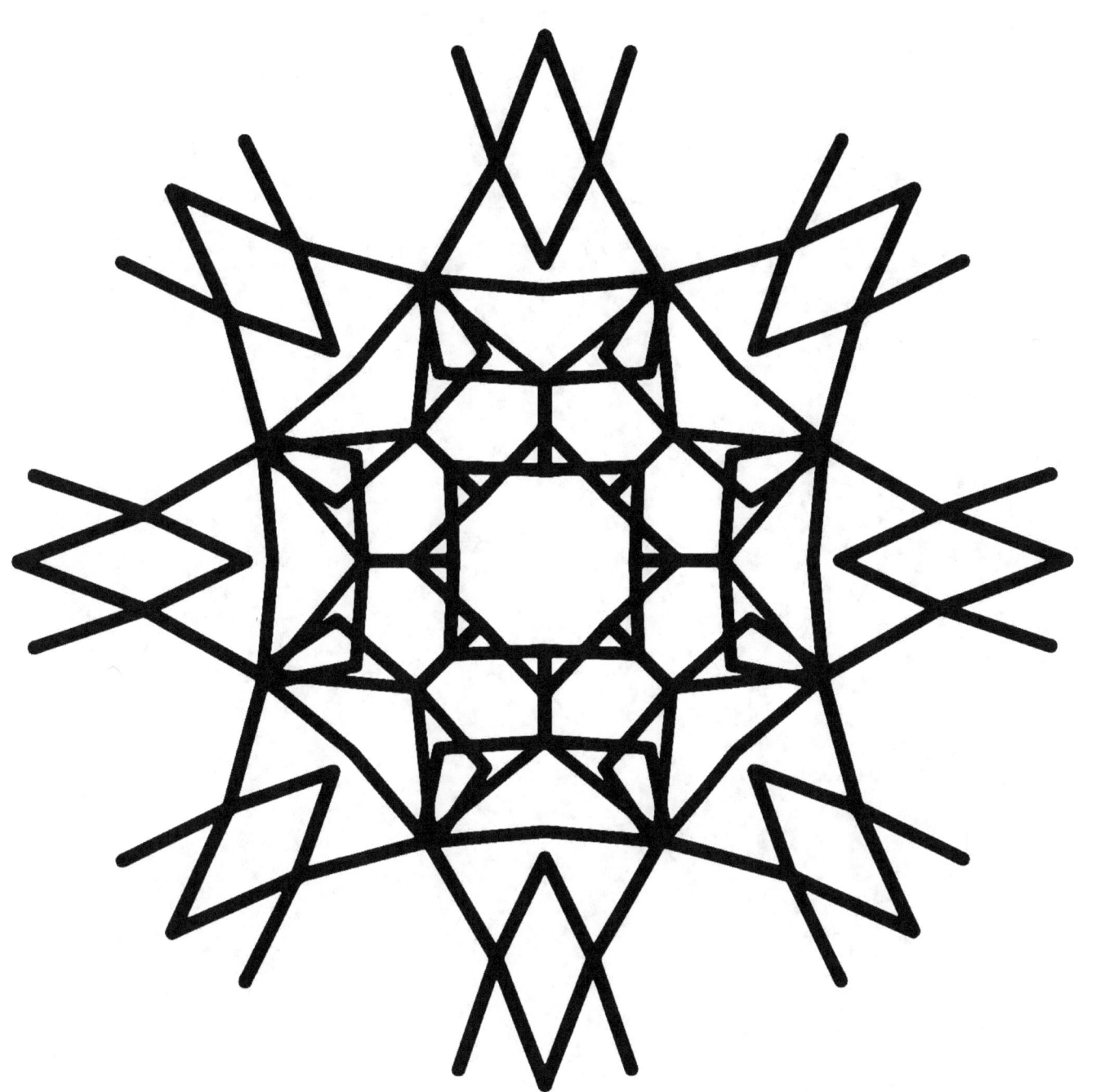

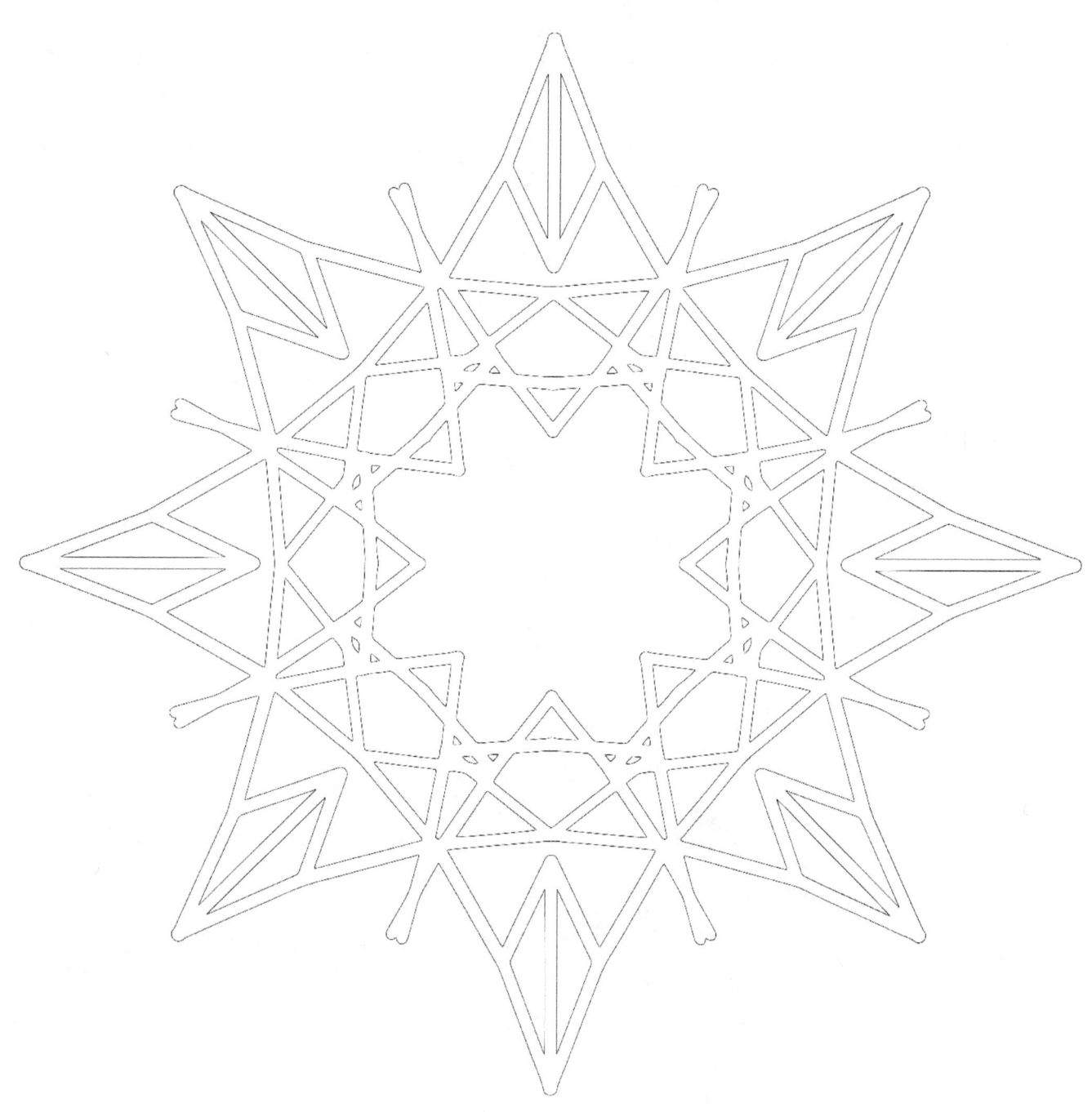

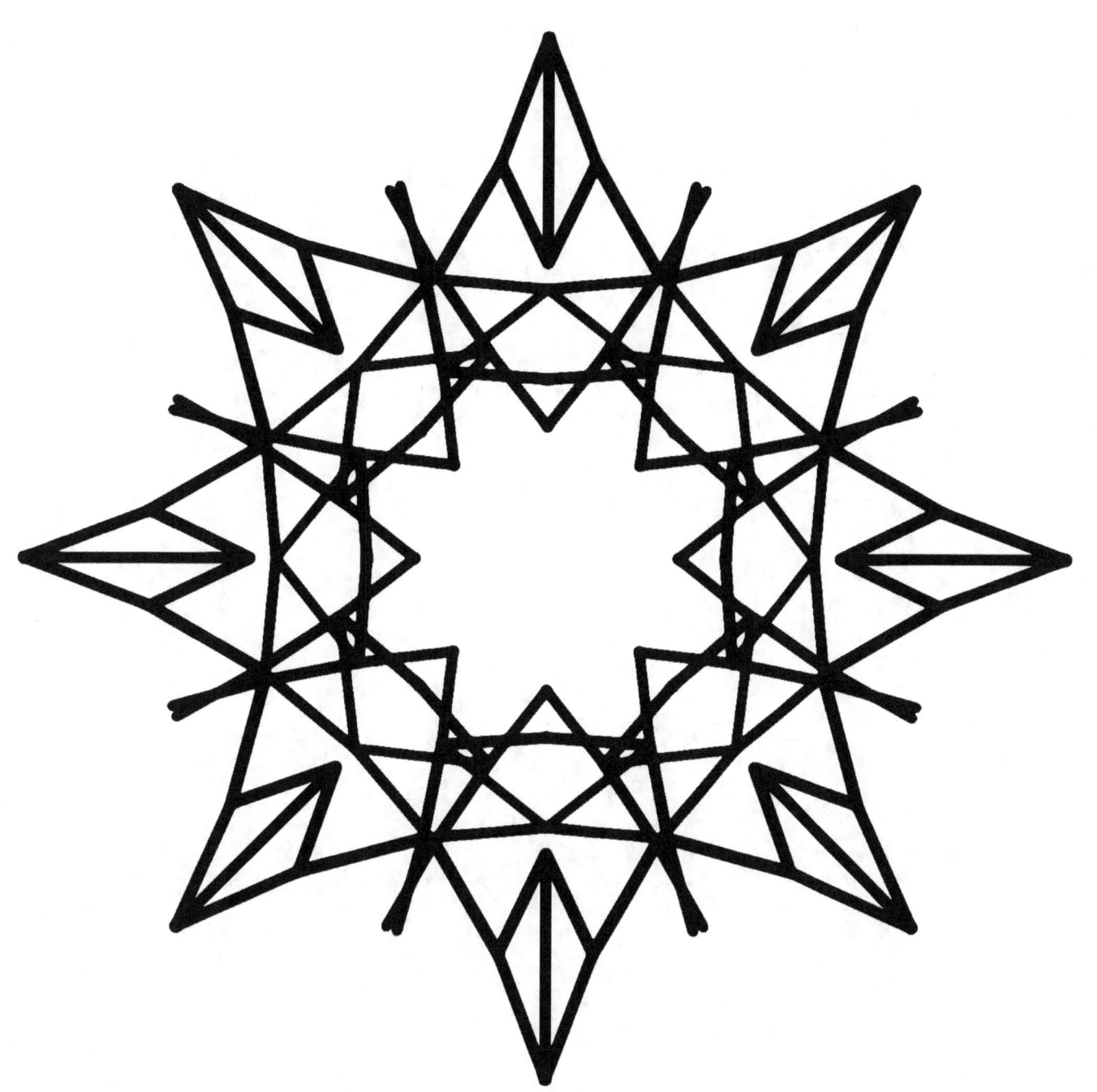

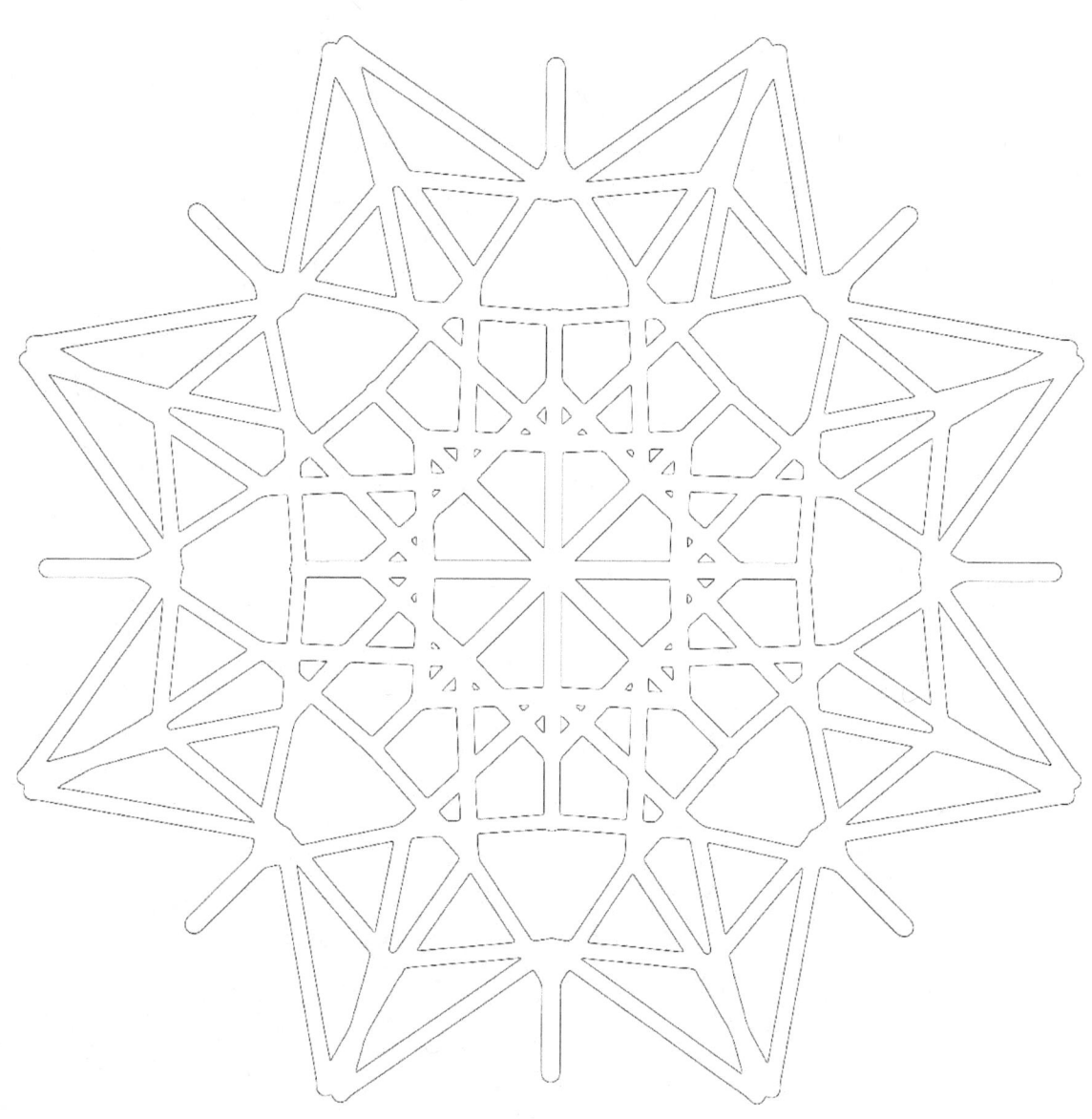

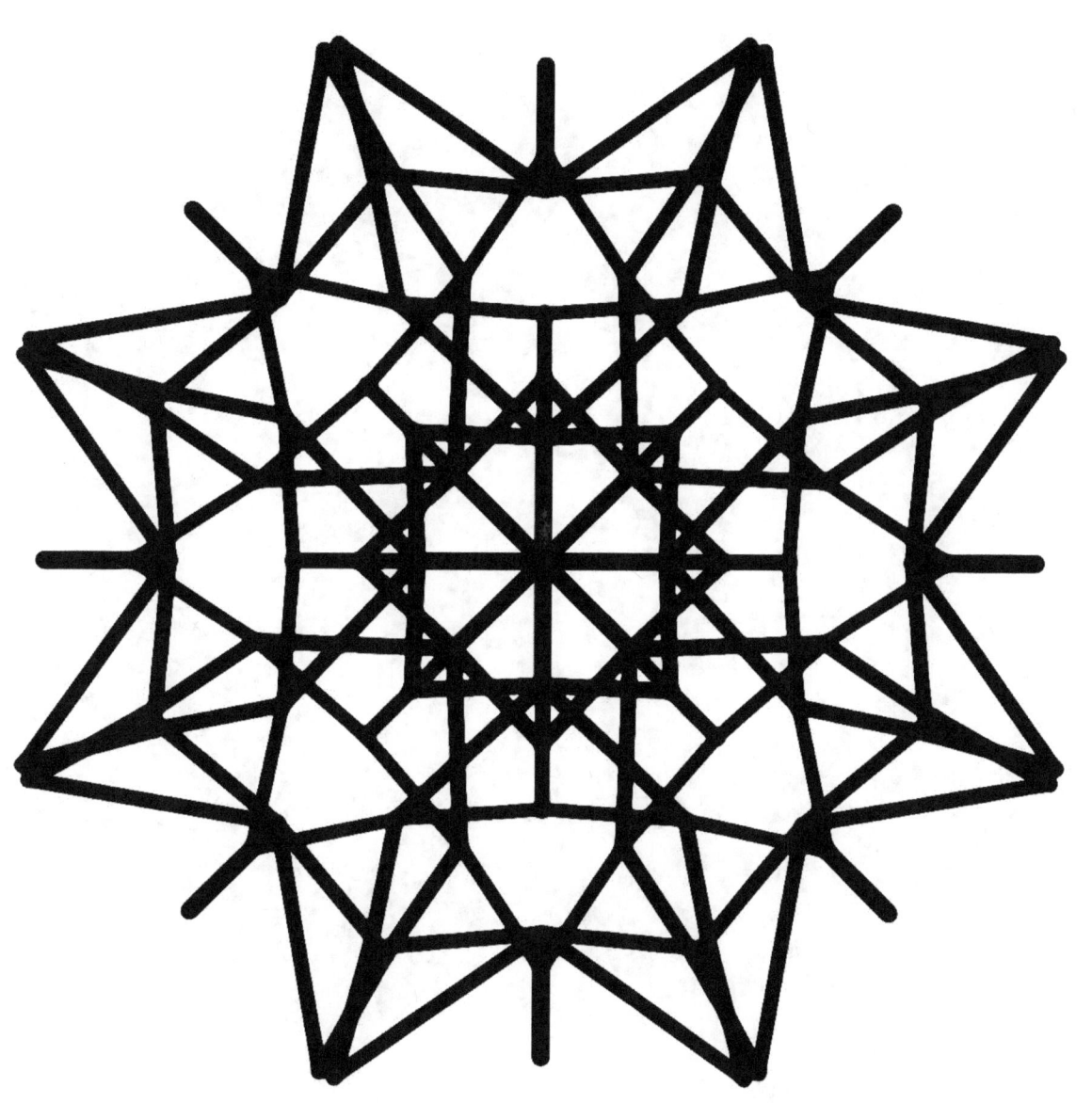

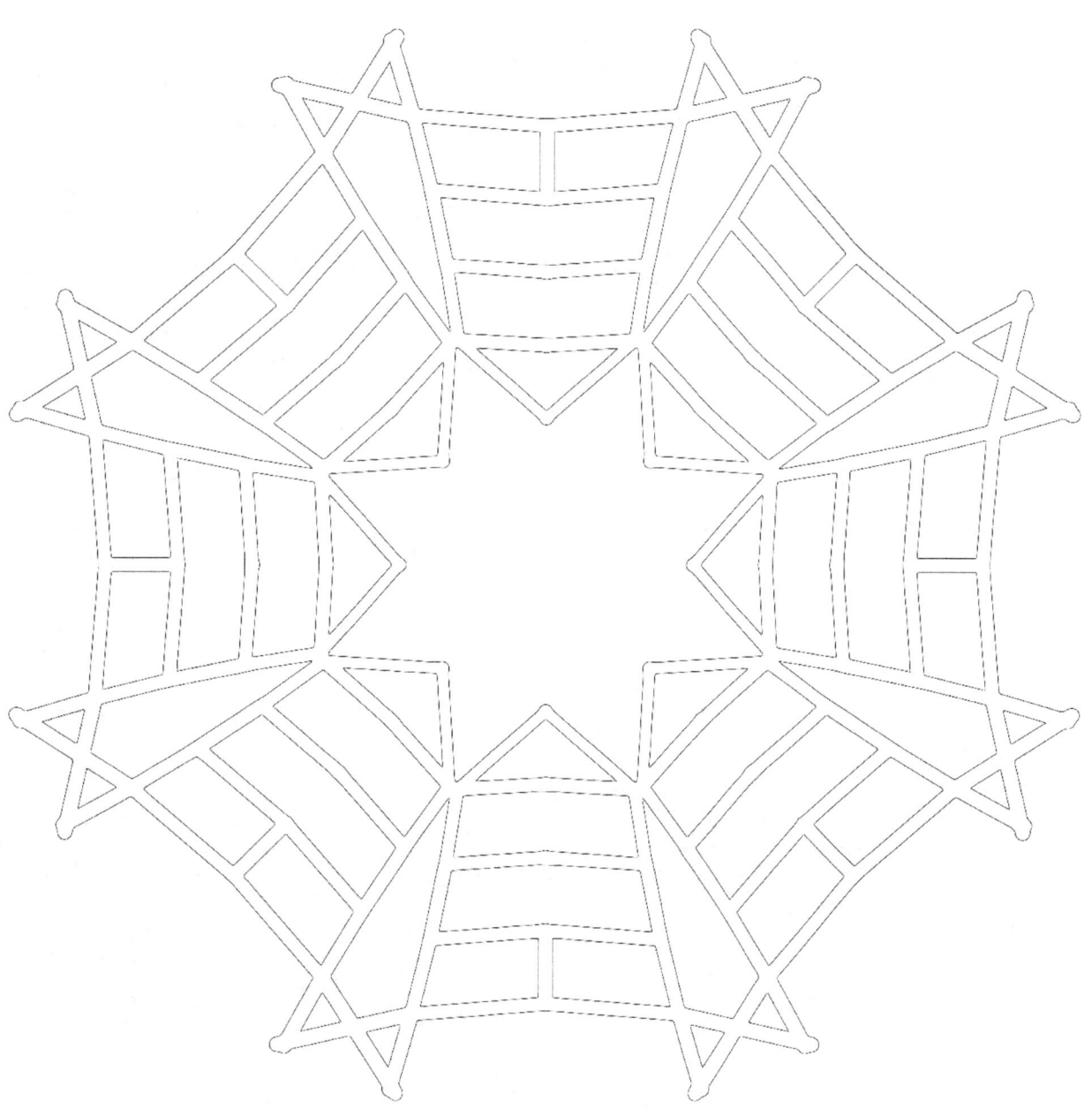

#kaleidoscopemandala19

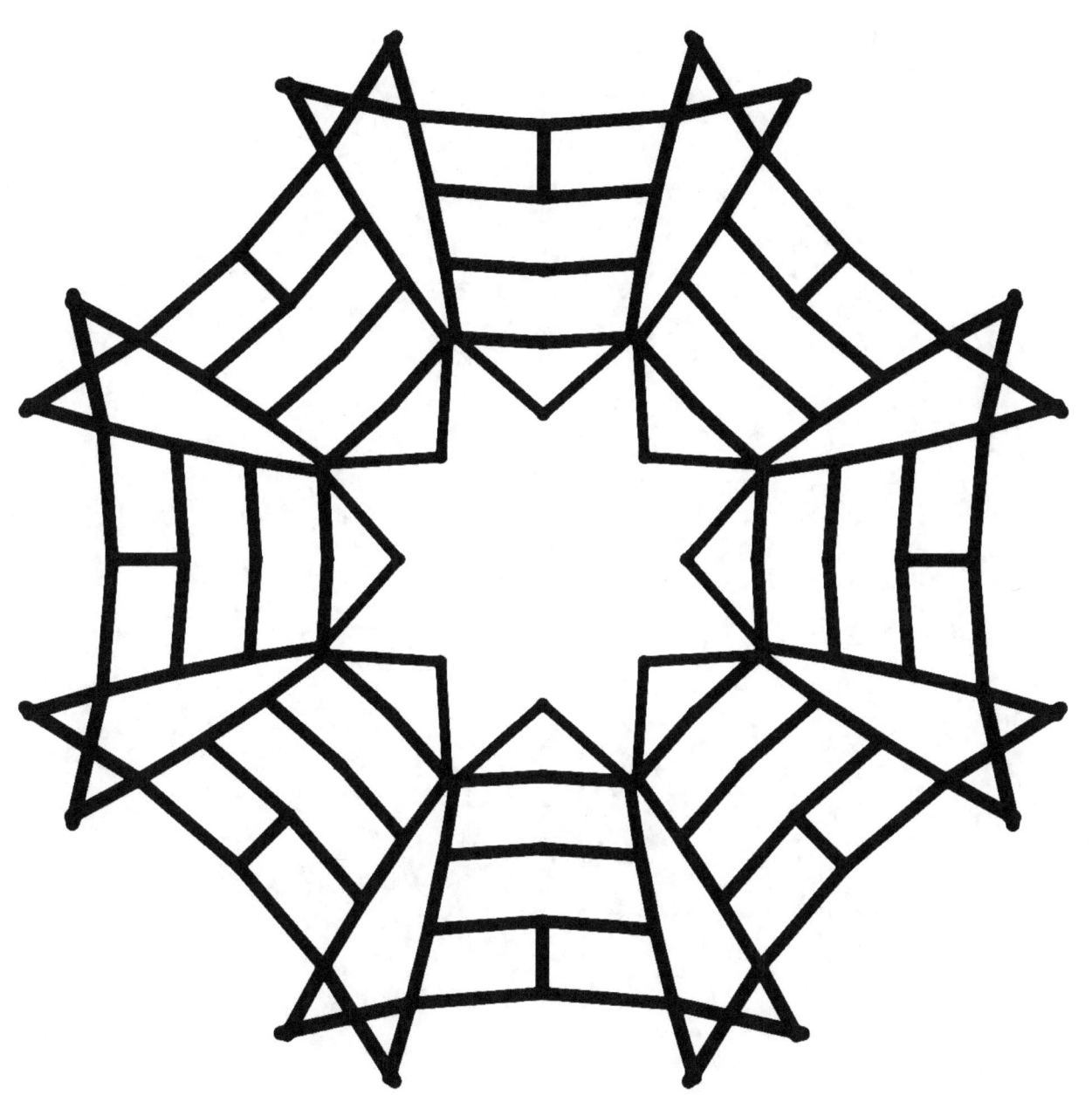

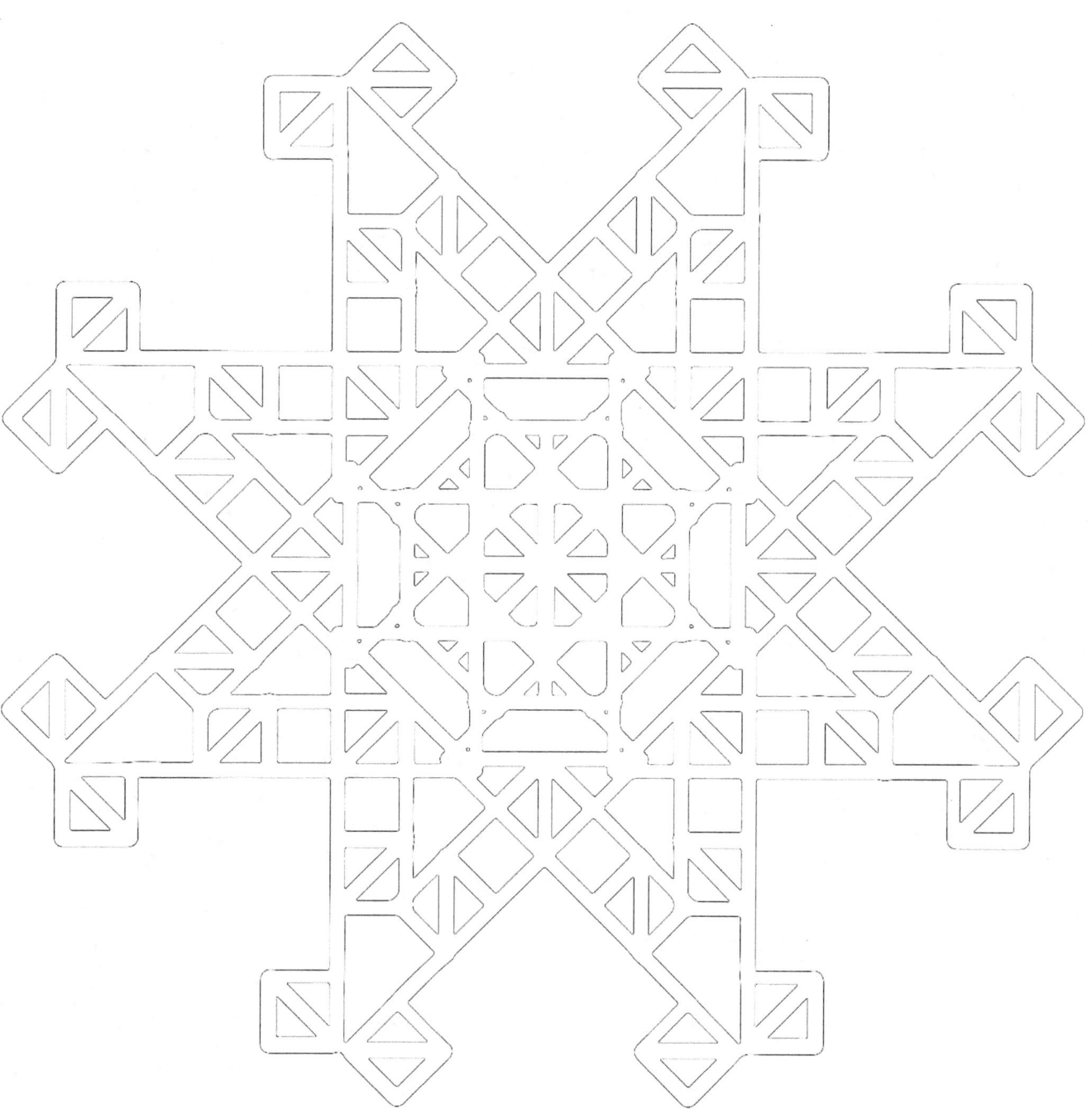

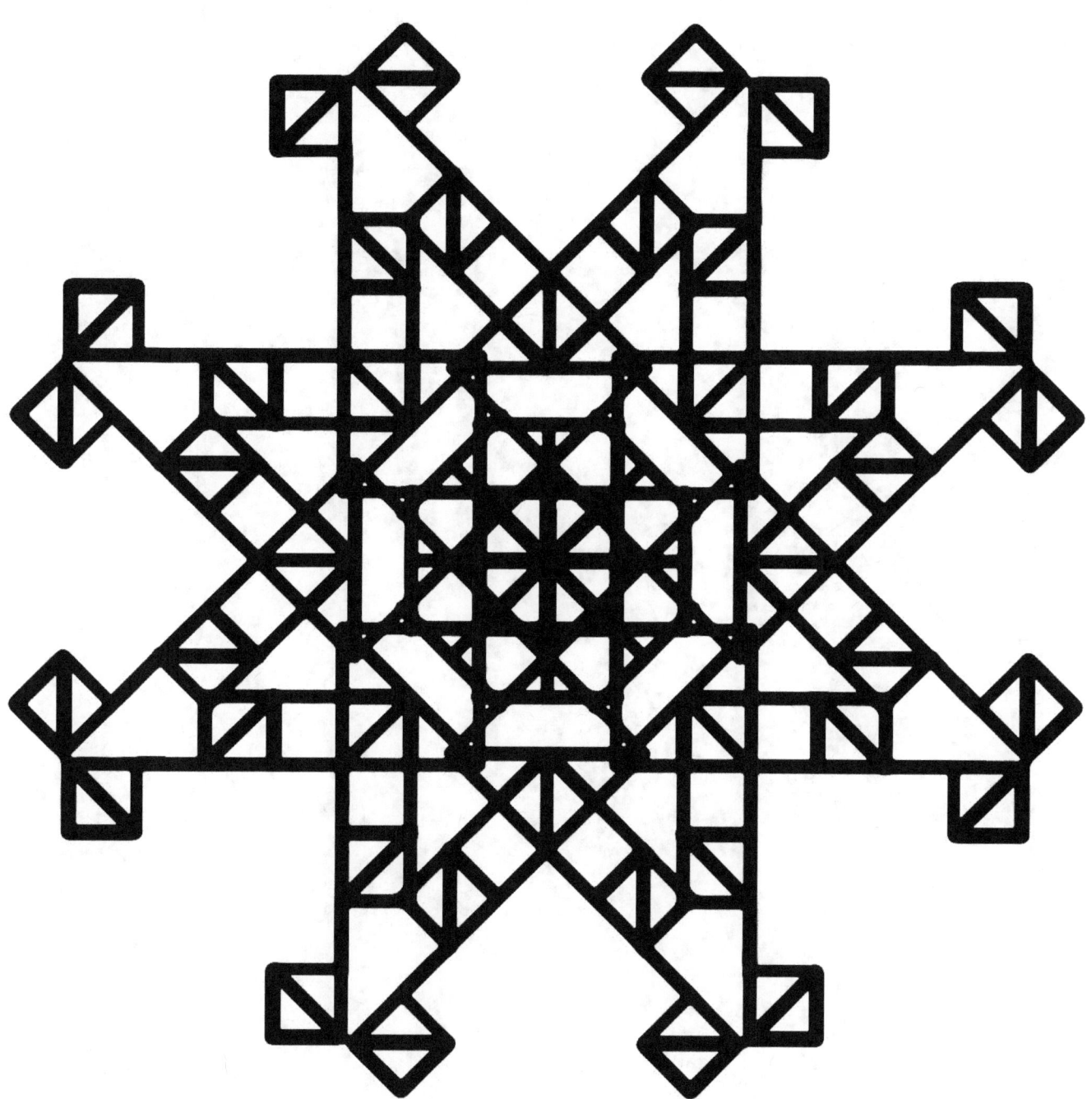

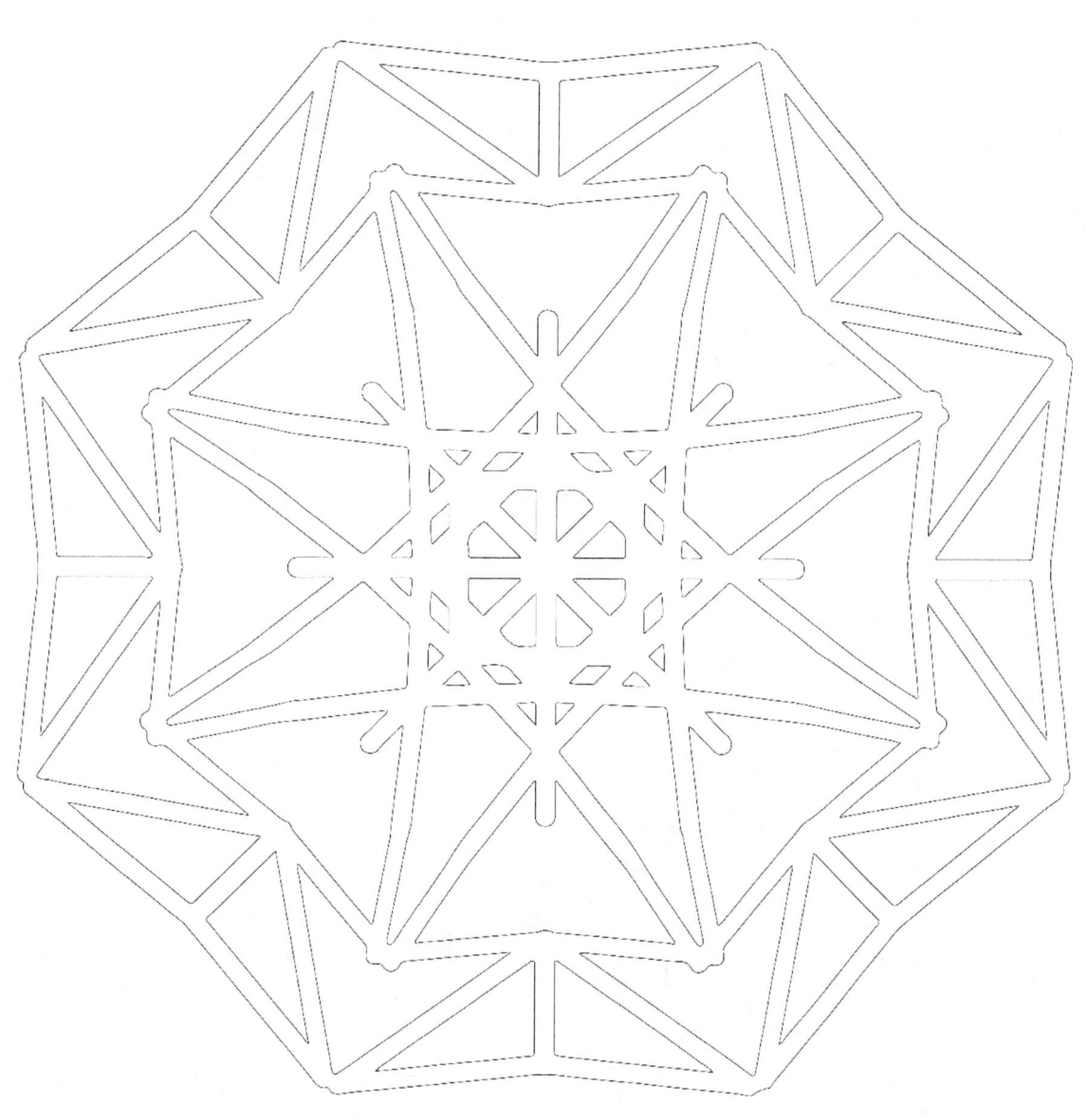

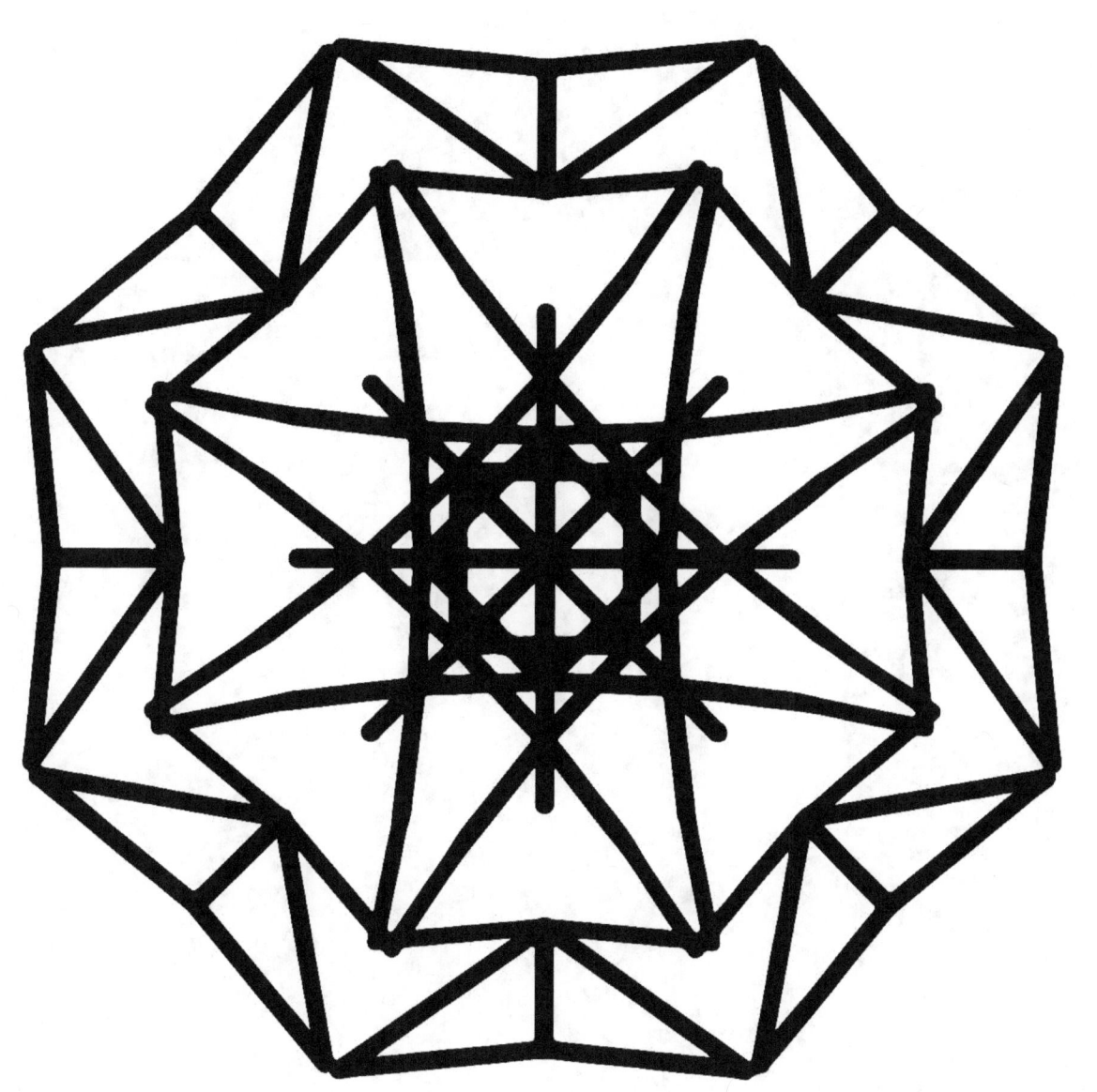

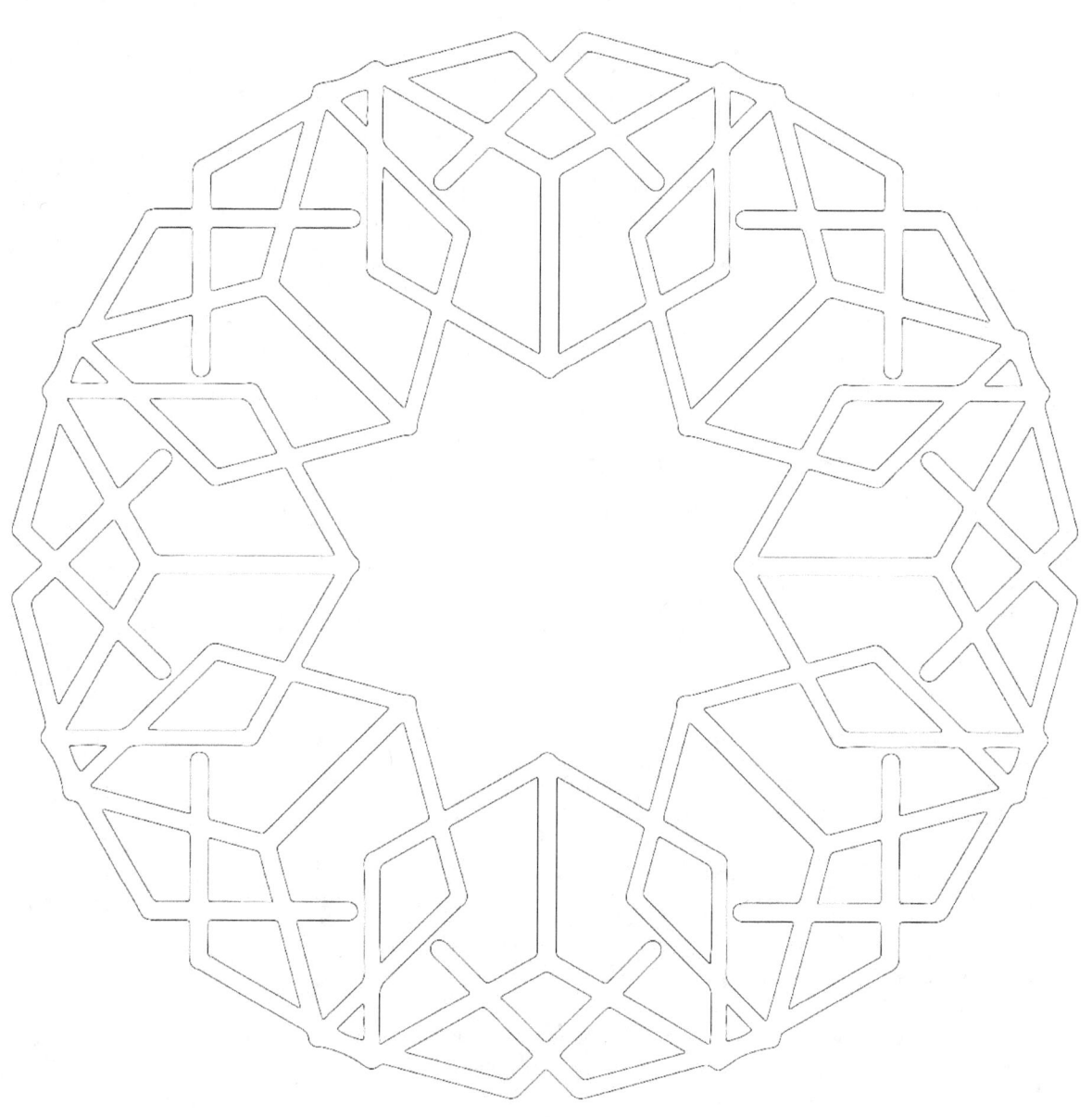

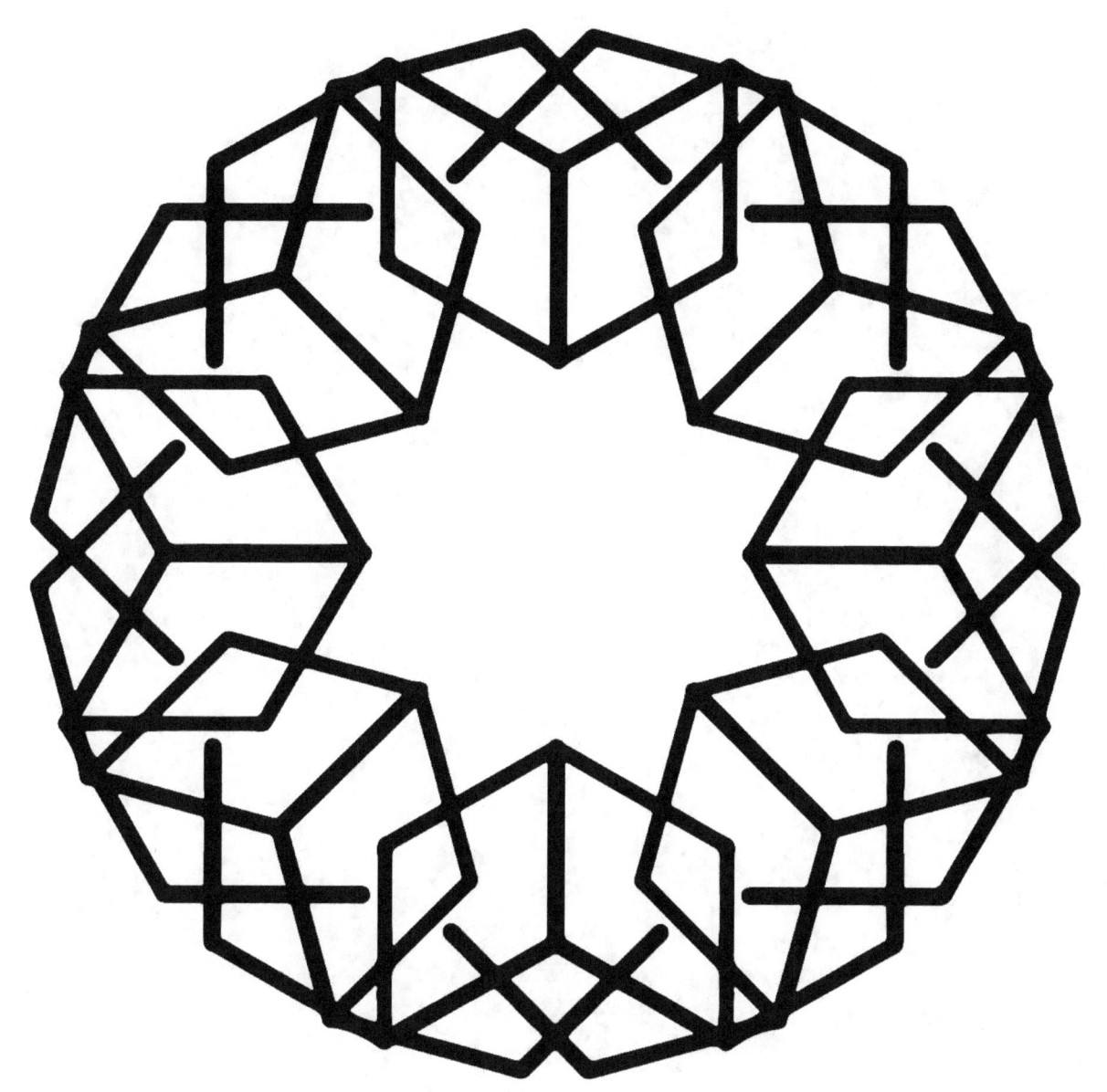

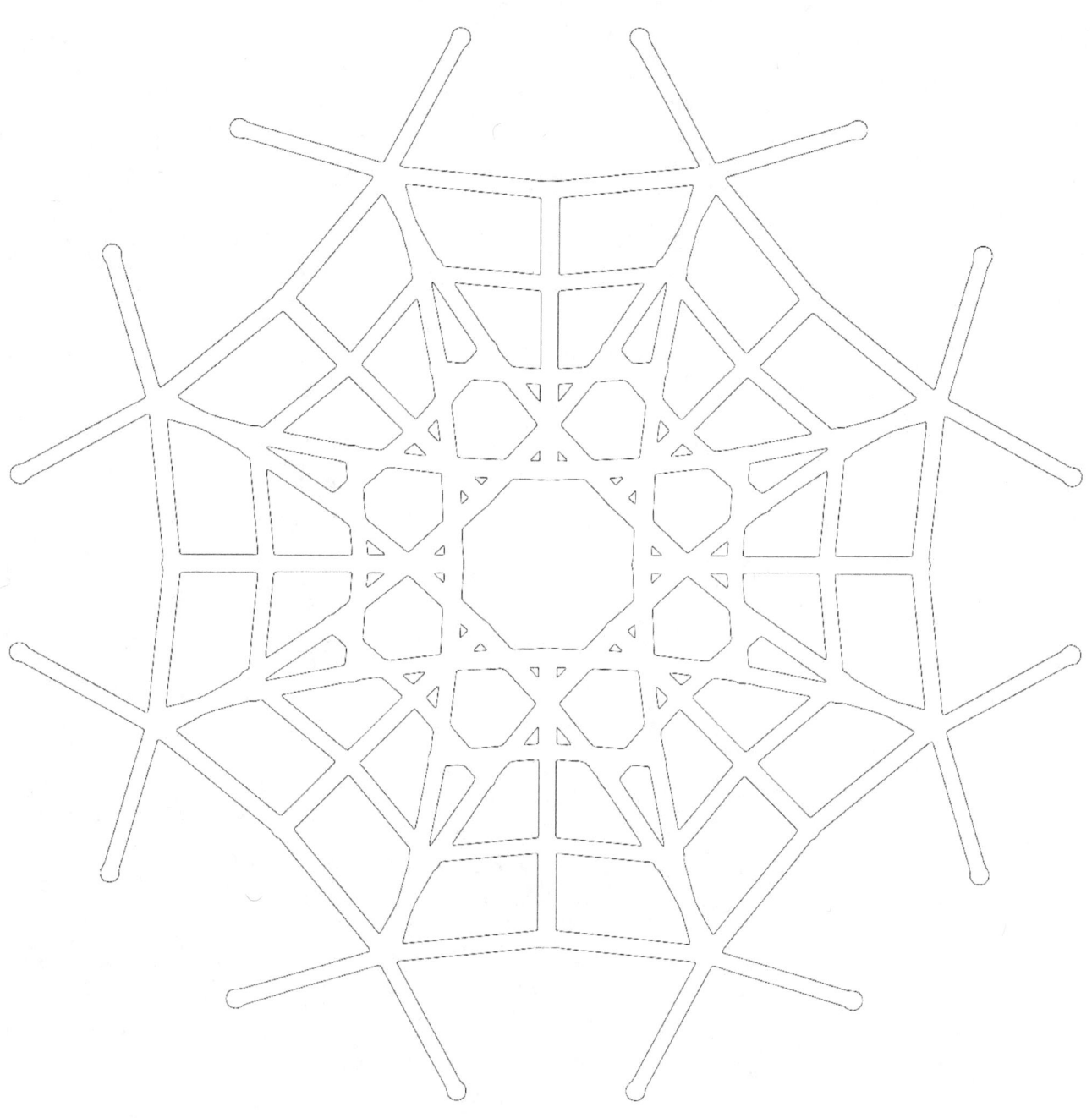

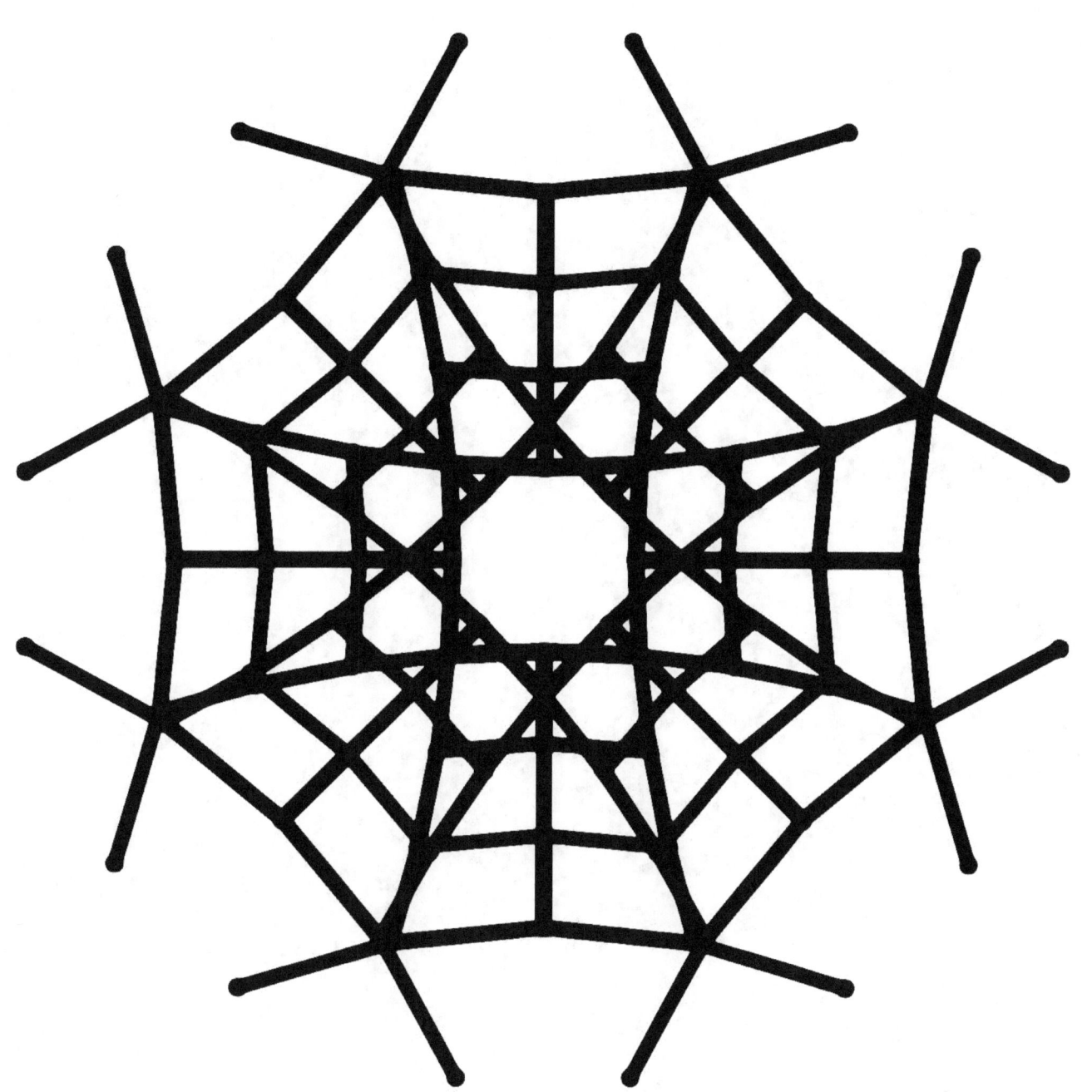

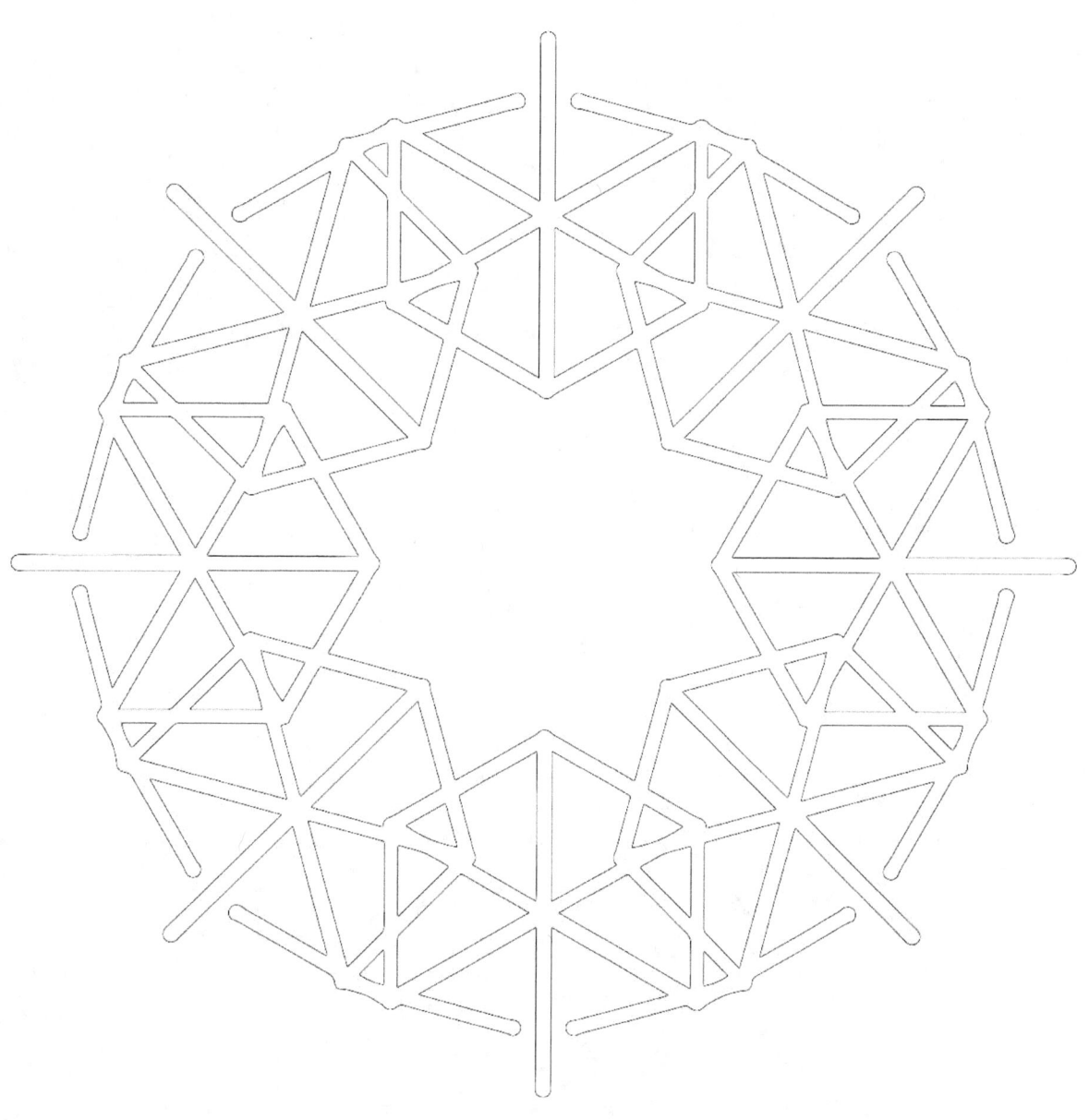

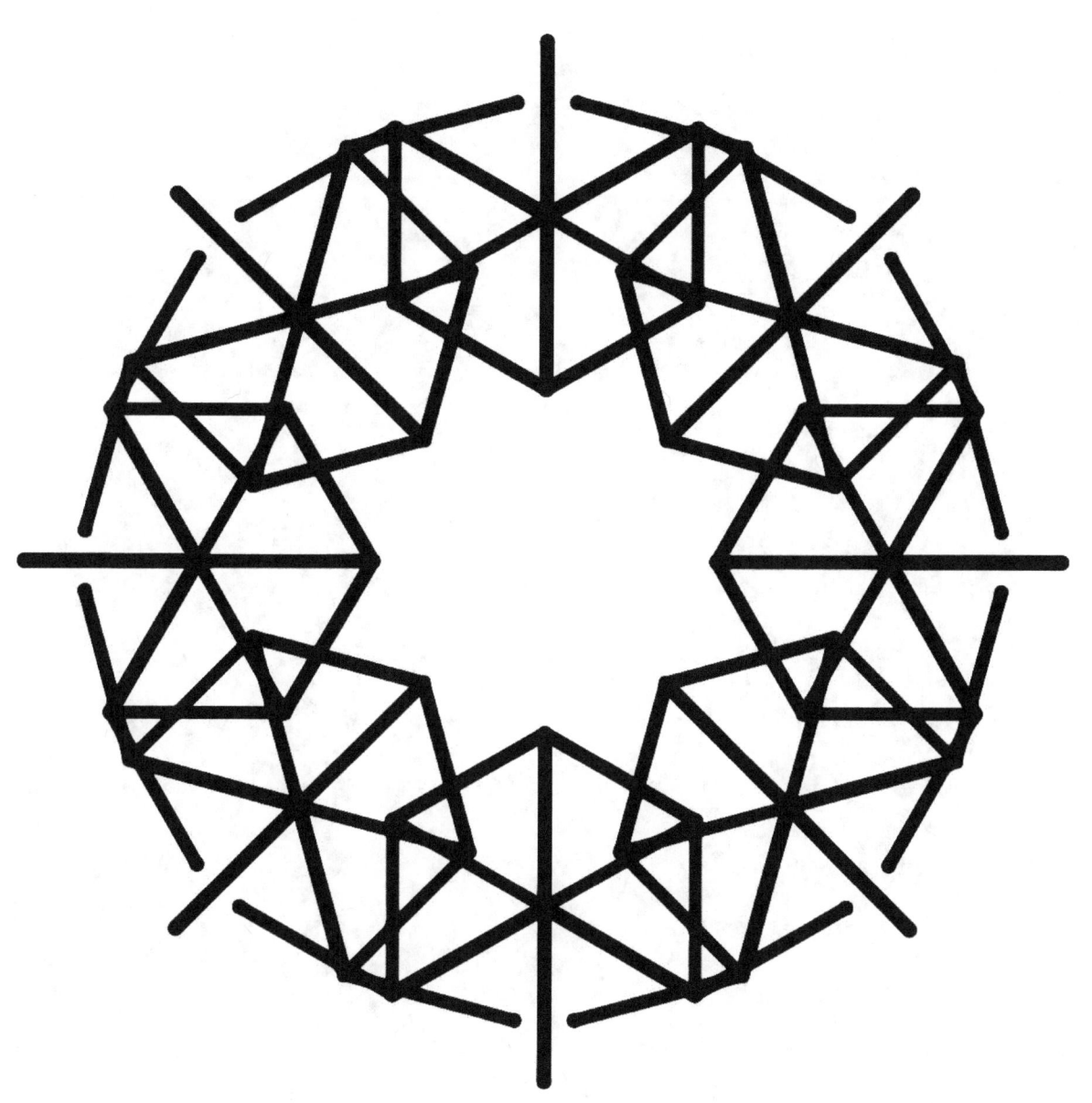

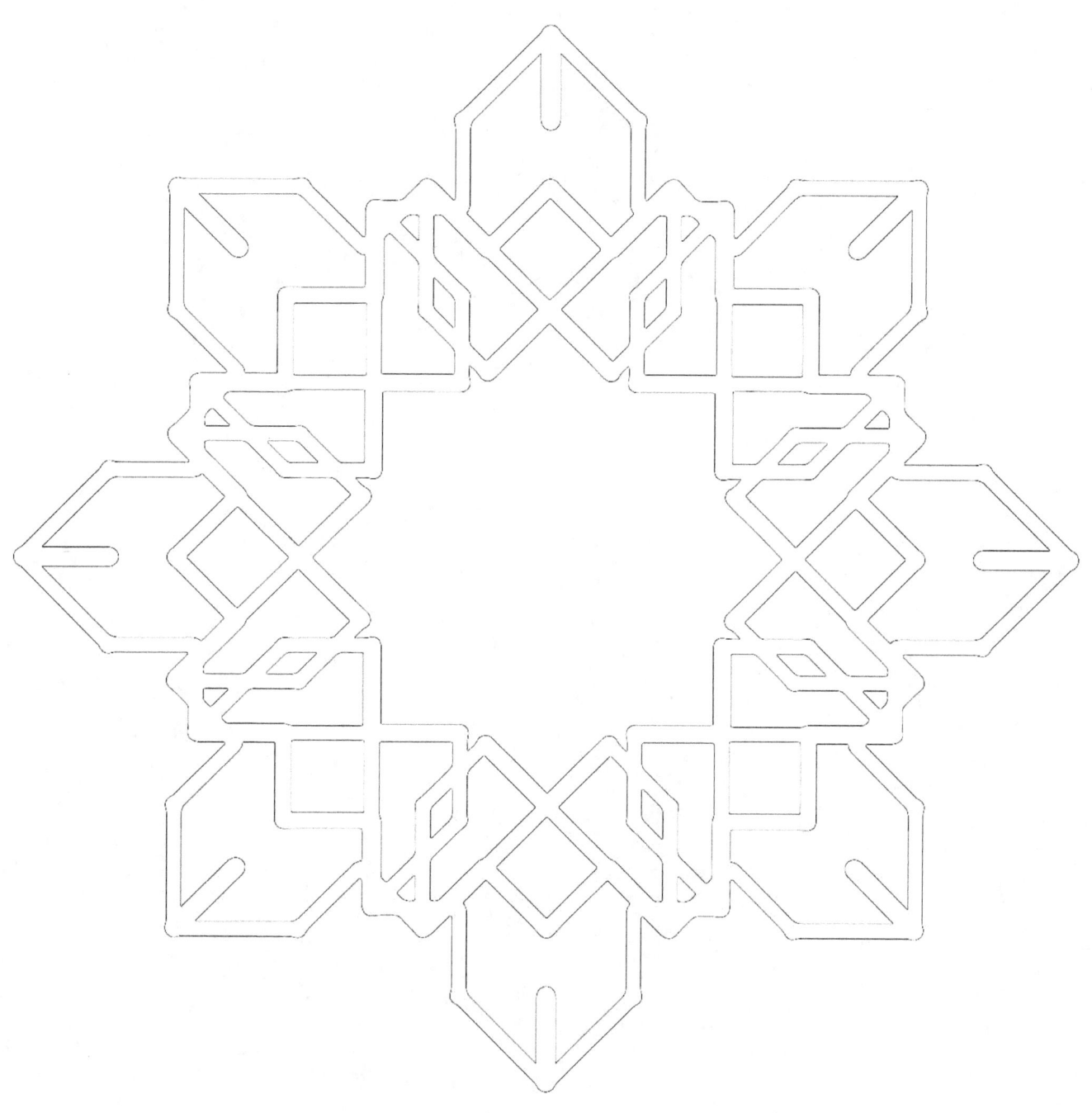

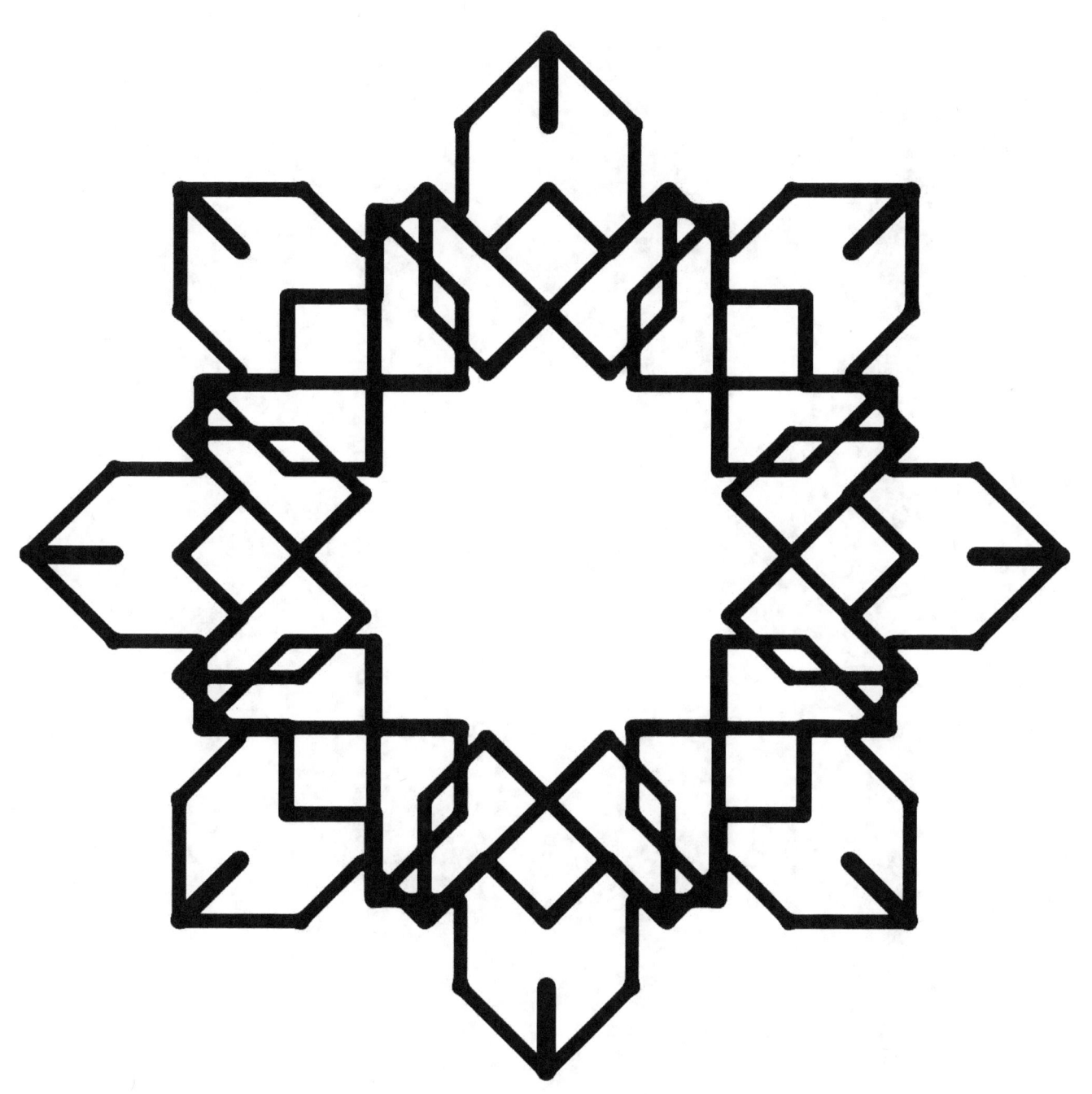